MuzMuz

Top 100
Working
Dogs

MJ Hutchinson, Andrea S Taher & Muz Taher

Contents

Questions

1. How is he / she at home, out of work?
2. Describe his or her character with 5 words..
3. What is his / her best quality?
4. What is his / her least desirable attribute?
5. Is he / she one of your favourite dogs of all time?
6. What is his / her favourite activity?
7. What is his / her biggest achievements?
8. Was he / she difficult to train?
9. What's your favourite offspring of his / her?
10. How heavy was or is he / she?
11. Where is your training club and decoys who helped him / her?
12. If you have the same dog again, what will you so different?
13. Is he / she social with people?
14. Any funny stories you want to share?
15. If you can change 1 thing about the dog, what would it be?
16. How was the dog like when he/ she as a puppy?
17. How was he / she like as he / she matured?
18. How are the dog's litter mates?
19. Is he / she social with other dogs?
20. Does the dog live in a house or a kennel?

Dog 1 – Tripp (BRN29582)

Owner: Christian Losiewski

1. How is he / she at home, out of work?

He is very active at home but has his own kennel he stays in

2. Describe his or her character with 5 words..

A dog that doesn't quit

3. What is his / her best quality?

He will fight until it's over

4. What is his / her least desirable attribute?

He can get over possessive and not give things up

5. Is he / she one of your favourite dogs of all time?

Yes one of my favorite dogs

6. What is his / her favourite activity?

He loves bite work and cooling off in the lake!

7. What is his / her biggest achievements?

Biggest achievement is staying on the bite when a suspect tried killing him saving officers lives

8. Was he / she difficult to train?

Extremely difficult to train the OUT hahaha

9. What's your favourite offspring of his / her?

My favorite offspring, this is a tough one. He just had a puppy with a PH-1 berry 2 daughter named Kyra and produced a really nice puppy we named Tripp II but overall Hawk is my favorite son of his. He is almost 19 months so I get to see how he turned out. Puppy is only 10 weeks old

10. How heavy was or is he / she?

60 pounds

11. Where is your training club and decoys who helped him / her?

He worked a lot with a trainer who trains secretive military operations for the army.

12. If you have the same dog again, what will you so different?

I would teach the out in a more relationship driven way.

13. Is he / she social with people?

Very neutral. Won't come up to be petted unless he's called over. He'd rather be looking for balls in the yard

14. Any funny stories you want to share?

So Tripp is actually the worst dog to collect from if you're the vet tech collecting him which is usually my girlfriend Katie Persons. He actually climbs the back of the bitch and will fall over on his side because he gets too excited and it's just very funny to watch him collect because he's ALL IN

15. If you can change 1 thing about the dog, what would it be?

I'd like for him to Out better so general obedience around the bite equipment

16. How was the dog like when he/ she as a puppy?

I did not have him as a puppy. I can only assume he was an asshole

17. How was he / she like as he / she matured?

I got to see him mature and he was a very intense dog that cared about nothing other than his work. First time he licked my face was 3 years after I got him

18. How are the dog's litter mates?

I don't know of any litter mates

19. Is he / she social with other dogs?

He is good with anything except an in tact male

20. Does the dog live in a house or a kennel?

He lives in his 8 x 8 run

Dog 2 - Duco II (BRN60)

Owner: Rob Seegers

I am amazed to see how many reactions I got on Duco, after all he's been dead for 18 years.

Duco wasn't a "wonderdog", he was just a crossbred Belgian Malinois without an official pedigree, not even DNA tested. The people who had him as a puppy would be pleased to know how famous he has become and that his genes are still to be found in many police dogs.

Bloodlines:

Thirty years ago the internet site www.bloedlijnen.nl didn't exist, a dog just needed to be KNPV and more important, practically qualified for the real job required. Some people were interested in, connection to breeding and lineage/bloodline of the Belgian Malinois.

When Duco more frequently was used to fertilize female dogs I tried to find out more on his background, but it didn't result in a 100 % certainty. This can only be done by DNA tested dogs. The lineage of the female dogs he fertilized wasn't certain as well. To breed dogs, it is important to know the lineage, this gives implications on heredity in order to prevent in-breeding. Mainly the cause of disability or diseases.

By using the site www.bloedlijnen.nl the registration of our crossbred dogs and their lineage has improved tremendously.

Everybody has his own opinion: we all have different views on beauty and favourite characteristics of a dog. The same with Duco, he was tested on hips, elbows and back, all of them were very good. But his photos weren't examined by The Hirschveld Stichting, nowadays normally done.

If the female dogs he fertilized were X-rayed? I am not sure, but when people made an appointment the female dogs were always 'super'. As owner of the male breeding dog you're depending on the given quality and lineage of the female dogs.

In the KNVP programme I have seen dogs more beautiful and better performing dogs than Duco. In exercises testing for will, tenacity, scent and courage he was a great performer, but he lacked in obedience and repetition. Of course he got his ph1. But the owners of female dogs kept coming for his offspring, even at old age. His pups were his best advertisement! Despite the numerous better looking, prize winning competition he never got out of business. He must have had his qualities there! His appearance in photos still charms people, but there are also people who have another opinion.

In short: he was a lovely, very healthy dog with a lot of spirit and character. But to breed healthy, good pups, you need a healthy good partner as well.

Breed:

Breeders need knowledge on character and behaviour in daily life settings. They need to make analysis on the weakness and strength aspects of their female dogs. The result of that should decide which male dog is suited for the job. Don't choose the owner, but the quality of the male dog. A bit of luck is always needed, but knowledge of genetics, feeding and caring is unmissable to breed better pups. Prevent in-breeding, it only leads to misery.

Years ago when I started training dogs we used dogs with a lot of natural talent and stamina. Instead of training them by stimulating good behaviour, as nowadays is done by rewarding them with strokes and balls, we used canes. Different times then. The sport has evolved for the better in a different type of dog.

Dog 3 - Montferland Dax (BRN15229)

Owner: Emily Houk and Marcel Alders

I am unsure as to where to begin in the story of Dax, and description of his character. I suppose the easiest beginning would be just that, at the beginning of his life.

Dax was bred by Marcel Aalders of Montferland K9 Services and working dog kennel van de Montferhoeve. He came from the combination of Django Sommers and Tess Aalders. This specific combination was a line-breeding on Duco II. The litter was born on August 7, 2006. Marcel can't exactly recall what Dax was like as a puppy, as this would've been 14 years ago now. However, Dax was the darkest in the litter and up until about 5 weeks he had one eye where the second eyelid stayed closed. This naturally corrected around 5 weeks of age. Dax was first pick from the litter by Leo Arts. Leo raised and trained Dax to his PH1 certificate of 413. Dax went for his PH1 on October 2, 2010, thus at 4 years of age. Shortly after getting his certificate, he was purchased by Tini van de Doelen. During the time of Tini owning Dax, he had several litters in the Netherlands. Dax lived in a kennel during this time as well. Around when Dax was 9, so maybe 2015, he was sold to Wilem van Buren in the US. I am unsure how long Wilem had him, or where he went after, but during his time in the US he changed hands several times before ending up with me in June of 2018, where he of course stayed until his passing 9 months later in February of 2019, at the age of 12. At the time I acquired Dax, he was owned by Jimmy Chilcott, and also who I co-owned Dax with. I will always be grateful to Jimmy for allowing me to own Dax, even if it was just a small fraction of his life.

Dax at home was interesting to say the least. Even at 11/12 the dog still had more drive than a lot of dogs I see. However, still he was pretty calm in the house. He would just lay around with a giant squeaky ball constantly crushing it over and over. Occasionally if the ball slipped loose he'd smash into things trying to get it again, but overall pretty chill in a house. He'd sleep in my bed, ride shotgun in my car, bar hopped with me. He was very chill, and very social outside of work. I'm actually convinced that if people saw him at home, they'd think he was a bad worker and just a pet.

Dax's character was in and of itself very special and unique. We have all seen nice dogs, but there was always something different about Dax that was difficult to explain. I think the only word that truly comes to mind, is heart. And I do not mean heart in the manner of emotional, love feelings, but in the manner of how an athlete just has heart for the game. Just sheer determination to succeed, yet enjoying every moment of it. He was the type of dog who would go through fire for anyone on the other side of the leash. He was a bit the type that when his mind was in something it was hard to change it otherwise and not much of a thinker either. When he would go down the field on an attack, it was all gas and he'd sort out what to do once he got there but not before.

Dax was also a good producer. He has produced some very notable offspring, including Dino Lindert, Biko Abbink,

Branco Aalders, Maddox (German police), Nico (US police, owned by Mike Lilley), Reza Mcgrotty, Kyra Carlisle, Rico jan Derksen, Luna Aalders, Nova Aalders, Monster Boren, Hippie Mud and many others.

Dax also had several very nice brothers as well. Off the top of my head, two come to mind. Astor was certified by Marcel Aalders with a score of 419 on his PH1. After certification, he was sold to the Austrian military. Egon was certified by Tonny Derksen with a score of 401 on his PH1. After certification, he went to the Dutch police in Nijmegen. I am sure there are several others, but can't remember more as it was a long time ago.

Dog 4 – Chaos (LOSH9255490)

Owner: Gunter Mertens

1. How is he / she at home, out of work?

Quite, easy at home, no noise, not nervous

2. Describe his or her character with 5 words..

Super fast high drive energetic dog with hard and stubborn character

3. What is his / her best quality?

Hard character, never fainting even after hard corrections

4. What is his / her least desirable attribute?

His fighting spirit makes him less fitted for sport.

5. Is he / she one of your favourite dogs of all time?

No, my favorite is Grimmer D'Ivar, one of his sons, he will be the better sport dog.

6. What is his / her favourite activity?

I guess mating, biting, eating.

7. What is his / her biggest achievements?

Always selected for Nationals, selections for grand prix and the 50th nvbk anniversary

8. Was he / she difficult to train?

Extremely difficult to train, because together with his hard stubbornness, he is never impressed by hard corrections.

9. What's your favourite offspring of his / her?

Grimmer D-litter in Sweden, Von Löwenfells litter, Statori S-litter, Croisé des Loups litters, in general all combinations with bloodlines from Chaos/Edden (Torky)

10. How heavy was or is he / she?

34 kg in competition, off season about 36 kg.

11. Where is your training club and decoys who helped him / her?

Hoboken Vinkenvelden Belgium, decoys Hans Verbruggen, Bart Bellon, civilians Geert Verbruggen, Willy Wuyts

12. If you have the same dog again, what will you so different?

Starting sooner as a young dog with more emphasis on control in obedience and in between exercises.

13. Is he / she social with people?

Indifferent to people, other animals and environmental distractions but not a pet dog! He does only allow people to touch him when he knows you, all the others he fights them and until now nobody dares to challenge him.

He's an honest dog but he will not accept a stranger to command or dominate him.

No handler aggression even during the hardest corrections.

14. Any funny stories you want to share?

He's too serious to have funny stories.

The trial in Torhout where he jumped on the fence during the send out, his kiss with the muzzle when a breeder wanted to help his female.

Some people left the training field when I came on the field with him.

Jumping over the fixed fence or palisade when somebody was leaning on it. Their faces were pale when he was growling during the jumps.

15. If you can change 1 thing about the dog, what would it be?

Less fighting, calmer grip.

16. How was the dog like when he/ she as a puppy?

He was an ugly pup, a monster, dirty character from the beginning.

17. How was he / she like as he / she matured?

He came very strong and mature.

18. How are the dog's litter mates?

No litter mates known.

19. Is he / she social with other dogs?

Only social with females, aggressive to other males

20. Does the dog live in a house or a kennel?

In a kennel, he would break the house down.

He's absolutely not the best sport dog, he's too hard and too stubborn.

Most people would never compete with such a dog but my aim is to compete with a hard strong dog and to show that it's possible.

It's my kind of dog and I will never accept a lesser dog to obtain more points.

From a genetic point of view, he passes his qualities to his offspring.

Several dogs from him are active or in preparation for Belgian Ring

and we have offspring from him in most venues of protection sports and LEwork.

We recognize a lot of him in his children, especially his honesty to the handler, speed in the attacks, muzzle work and object guarding.

He did for the moment about 100 trials in NVBK, 6 years competition with 4 years in the highest category, each year qualified for the national championships. (5th in 2013, 8th in 2014,10th in 2015 and 6th in 2016, 4th in 2017, 8th in 2018)

Several wins in the highest category, mostly difficult trials, his last year he still won two trials at the age of 10.

Best exercise is the independent work during object guarding (decoy and muzzle work on civilians), never lost his object in the trials.

Dog 5 – **Bolo** (BRN23915)

Owner: Ferrie Bernst

1) How is he at home, out of work.

At home it is a quiet dog that is nice and quiet in the house, when visitors come he is vigilant

2) Describe his character with 5 words.

Small size, big in character

3) What is his best quality

Being able to switch from home situation to work situation

4) What is his least desirable attribute?

The garden hose

5) Is he one of your favourite dogs of all time?

If I look purely at my own dogs for sure, although my current female dog is also super.

6) What is his favourite activity?

Bite exercises without a doubt.

7) What are his biggest achievements?

When he was with me of course his PH1 certificate, several arrests were made to the police.

8) Was he difficult to train?

No that was easy, he was a hard dog who did everything to bite. That sometimes made it difficult.

9) What is your favourite offspring of his?

Unfortunately there are not that many offspring yet, hopefully a litter is on the way.

10) How heavy was he?

He is around 32 kilos

11) Where is your training club and decoys who helped him?

My club is "PHV Ons Genoegen in Helmond". decoys are too many to mention but would like to thank them all!

12) If you have the same dog again, what will you do differently?

In terms of dogs I will not want otherwise, I will train in a different way and not all focus on biting.

13) Is he social with people?

When he was with me, although you had to keep an eye on him, now that he is with the police he is social towards his own people.

14) Any funny stories you want to share?

Yes looking back it is funny, but at the time it was not funny. Bolo has sometimes mistaken himself for biting in a dark space between the handler and the helper. But he realized soon enough that he had caught the wrong one.

15) If you can change 1 thing about the dog, what would it be?

That he was slightly darker in color.

16) How was the dog like when he was a puppy.

As a puppy it was a puppy that quickly got angry. There is a movie circulating somewhere on social media that he attacked a shoe at 7 weeks.

17) How was he like as he matured?

Then he calmed down a bit and became clearer in his head.

18) How are the dog's litter mates?

I dare not say it in terms of character, but I do know that a nest brother is certified.

19) Is he social with other dogs?

NO! Only with own dogs.

20) Does the dog live in a house or a kennel?

Both

Dog 6 – Tuco (BRN22693)

Owner: Stacey Beller

1) How is He at home, out of work?

Very good in crate and in the house. Very much my dog but lives great with rest of family. Almost a damn lap dog.

2) Describe his best quality in 5 words?

Always has my Back 110%

3) What is his best quality?

Tenacity and drive to get whatever he is after. He has done some incredible things in PSA trials and nothing has ever stopped him from getting a bite. I can also trust him to bounce back very quickly from any correction and be ready to work instantly.

4) What are his least desirable attribute?

Hair trigger if any dog bows up to him, not dogs just out and about he is neutral. He won't ever go after another dog. However, He has zero tolerance for any dog who thinks they are going to dominate him or even try and show him up. He doesn't just fight he explodes on them. So we keep a close eye on those loose dogs. He is also a resource guarder little asshole will die for his food or crate area.

5) Is he your favorite dog of all time?

Yes, he has been. The best dog I have ever owned. Not a dog in the world I would trade him for.

6) What is his favorite activity?

Anything that will bring a reward. He has fantastic hunt and retrieve and just has always loved working for toy. He may love competition more than me as he is always game.

7) What is his biggest achievement?

2016 PSA3 National Champion at 3 years old, PSA3 at 5 years old, he is the 20th PSA3 dog out of 24 in the world. Should have been sooner but suffered a fractured jaw and had substantial time off recovering. One he returned to competition he closed out his PSA3 in 2 trial weekend.

8) Was he difficult to train?

No, quite easy. I trained certain behaviors in a week or two that he retained through his entire career. I try to be very clear on any task like guard or transport or change of positions etc. example, he learned guard on me, in my suit, then transport with me in a suit in a matter of a few sessions. Then we build that on decoy.

9) What is your favorite offspring of his?

Man, that is a tough question and I don't want to hurt any of his pup owners feelings. I have only had two litters with him. I have turned down numerous stud requests, not because I did not think the females were not worthy but I think there are to many people breeding Malinois at this point and I don't need the money, if I can't monitor pup placement or where they end up I am not interested. That being said, I love his pup Miller. Dog is very hard to control as his drive is over the top. He always has outstanding grip. Fearless. Just a super nice dog. Not big but mighty, I love a female pup Brew owned by Josh Kirby also, she is very clear headed and first pup to achieve PSA1 title from his first litter. But really there are more pups in his two litters I wish I had back right now to train because I love the tenacity and work ethic of them all. I love the handlers who train them and do their best. To close this out, I don't think a dog should be judged solely on the pups they produce especially when one doesn't want the dog spread all over the place. In the Us it is a huge problem with people thinking they want a Mal and being a bitch about it and sending it to the pound.

10) How heavy is he?

Currently 70 pounds, not a big dog but stocky. Know some like bigger dogs but in PSA they have so many jumps hard impacts I prefer a normal size dog.

11) Where is your training club/decoys?

K9 working dogs of Dallas is our club, Dallas Texas. club decoys that have helped the most are of course Khoi Pham training director, Josh Kirby, Tim Akers, Darrick Rose, Colten Erbe Chad Vivanco, Kimberly Balega the list goes on grateful for them all.

12) If I had the same dog again what would I do differently?

Train certain behaviors earlier. PSA has a lot of directional attacks, Tuco does well on Directional however at higher levels it is tough. These behaviors can be imprinted earlier for better success.

13) Is he social?

Yes very. I can trust him with people and small children, he seems to know to chill with young kids and actually gravitates to them. I have videos of letting a 7 year old girl send him for bite. Also letting anyone pet him at club. If you push him he will warn you. He will also bite anyone I tell him to. It is imprinted at a young age. Including myself.

14) Funny stories?

During a level 2 fended off he could have went around a 6 foot fence intend he went up and flipped over and came up biting. I will send you the photo sequence if you have not seen it.

15) If I could change one thing about him?

Sometimes in trial his drive get hard to control. Often wish in certain situations I could tone that down. However then what fun would that shat be right? The thrill of the game and seeing if you can control your dog in all situations is what makes PSA fun. Controlled aggression!

16) How was Tuco as a puppy?

Ready to work when he came off the plane from the Netherlands. Always ready to work and literally potty trained fast, crate trained fast. Was a resource guarder like I said. BIt the shat out of me at 6 months over food and he met Jesus that day. Lolol otherwise other than a few bouts of him trying to dominate me he was easy.

17) How has he matured?

Love the dog. Dog will do anything for me. I can look him in the eye and know he knows exactly what to do when I give him a command. We have spent so many hours training he is like a third hand. Travels well. Over half of out compelitions were as far as 200-600+ miles from home He treats all places like he has been there forever. Has excellent nerve as well. Perfect dog for me. Wish other people who have struggled with dogs could own a great dog and it would change them. Many Dogs do not get PSA3 until they are 7, 8 years old because it is so difficult. To win national champion at 3 and achieve PSA3 at 5 is a great feat.

18) How are his litter mates?

They are all in the Netherlands, one is a PH1 working for the Dutch military, one passed from testicular cancer at a young age but was awesome. Those are the only ones I know about.

19) Is he social with other dogs?

Neutral like I said earlier. But will fight like an asshole if provoked.

20) Does he live in the house?

He lives in the house. I consider him our PPD also with control.

Celiks Home Tuco

Dog 7 – Scaramouche (BRN8324 & LOSH544061)

Owner: Partrick Heiremans

1. How is he / she at home, out of work?

He was social to the people he lived with,suspicious of strangers,and would attack a civilian by order of his boss. Sports dogs don't all do this, they're more the exception than the rule.

2. Describe his or her character with 5 words..

Self-assured willingness to work, tenacity, sharp intelligence, toughness, alertness, cleverness, courage,

3. What is his / her best quality?

Fetch (at the age of 5 months he fetched everything). After changing teeth directly on the attack suit for adult dogs .

4. What is his / her least desirable attribute?

The last season I played it, cup at the championship for best obedience and jumping.

5. Is he / she one of your favourite dogs of all time?

Ofcourse born and raised with me .

6. What is his / her favourite activity?

He loved to train.

7. What is his / her biggest achievements?

First season (cat 3) 2nd in the championship of Belgium. Second season as cat 2 Champion of East-Flanders and both Flanders. Later in cat 1, 2nd place Championship later after adjusting the rules otherwise he would have been champion .

8. Was he / she difficult to train?

There are no easy dogs, I put everything higher and further to never lose points at a race. Guarding always had to be trained as well.

9. What's your favourite offspring of his / her?

There have been some dogs who also played matches.

10. How heavy was or is he / she?

32-kg

11. Where is your training club and decoys who helped him / her?

Nidendog Denderwindeke the club is no longer active , attacker Patrick Geeroms (person who was there on videotape TV)

12. If you have the same dog again, what will you so different?

The dog had so many good qualities that I would now use them even better.

13. Is he / she social with people?

I could take the dog to the vet without a muzzle, he was completely under my control, but still he was suspicious of strangers.

14. Any funny stories you want to share?

My first provincial championship said a friend who had a good cat 1 dog to play at that time, don't play this game next week is the championship cat 3 and here your dog is going to be disrupted for next week. There was an attack and while the dog was biting the attacker was beaten very hard with a whip next to the dog. Scaramouche just bit that attack and my friend unloaded his dog prematurely, was pretty funny.

15. If you can change 1 thing about the dog, what would it be?

He had an ear that he had damaged in his youth so she was not straight so I would like to see this differently.

16. How was the dog like when he/ she as a puppy?

Very quiet,self-confident.

17. How was he / she like as he / she matured?

Still very calm and self-confident

18. How are the dog's litter mates?

Together with scaramouche there were also 2-pups with trainers, also these dogs could place them for the championship cat 3, so with the 20 best dogs of the then +- 100 competition dogs which was very exceptional.

19. Is he / she social with other dogs?

Never had problems with my own dogs, with other dogs I never released him.

20. Does the dog live in a house or a kennel?

He lived in a kennel

Dog 8 – Jari (BRN24588)

Owner: Hein Van Gaalen

1. How is he / she at home, out of work?

Relaxed around the house, social to his own family, not social to strangers.

2. Describe his or her character with 5 words..

Unstoppable drive to work, always alert, tough dog, serious, no fear.

3. What is his / her best quality?

Bite is very hard, great searching skills.

4. What is his / her least desirable attribute?

Has none.

5. Is he / she one of your favourite dogs of all time?

Yes

6. What is his / her favourite activity?

Biting

7. What is his / her biggest achievements?

PH1 425 points, real life matches.

8. Was he / she difficult to train?

Yes, he is always high in drive, when he is not allowed to do something, he is not afraid to bite you.

9. What's your favourite offspring of his / her?

Kuro, Jan Sieuw

10. How heavy was or is he / she?

35 kilogram

11. Where is your training club and decoys who helped him / her?

Police Dog Club Zeddam, Decoys: Rob Tomberg, Ralph Hendriksen, Ivo Hoevers.

12. If you have the same dog again, what will you so different?

Put more pressure on the dog from a young age.

13. Is he / she social with people?

For his own people.

14. Any funny stories you want to share?

Nothing funny about him.

15. If you can change 1 thing about the dog, what would it be?

Would be good if he was less hard to train.

16. How was the dog like when he/ she as a puppy?

Very sweet and spontaneous puppy.

17. How was he / she like as he / she matured?

Difficult to train, tough, one man army.

18. How are the dog's litter mates?

Same as Jari, all working dogs with the police dogs and the army.

19. Is he / she social with other dogs?

Yes social to other animals.

20. Does the dog live in a house or a kennel?

In the kennel

Dog 9 – Keith (KC AR03300601)

Owner: Ursi Furter

1. How is he / she at home, out of work?

Keith is a workaholic, although he can switch off he's always on the move and if not trained daily he's not fully happy.

2. Describe his or her character with 5 words..

Fast, extreme driven, loyal.

3. What is his / her best quality?

Learns super fast and his speed.

4. What is his / her least desirable attribute?

He can be slightly hectic.

5. Is he / she one of your favourite dogs of all time?

He is the favourite and best dog in my life.

6. What is his / her favourite activity?

Bitework.

7. What is his / her biggest achievements?

FCI's and FMBB qualified.

8. Was he / she difficult to train?

No but he learns bad stuff too fast too.

9. What's your favourite offspring of his / her?

He's a police dog.

10. How heavy was or is he / she?

He's around 30kg.

11. Where is your training club and decoys who helped him / her?

My helper is in Belgium and Holland.

12. If you have the same dog again, what will you so different?

Make less drive, keep him calmer and train with food more.

13. Is he / she social with people?

Only people he knows.

14. Any funny stories you want to share?

He killed a couple of deers.

15. If you can change 1 thing about the dog, what would it be?

Be slightly calmer.

16. How was the dog like when he/ she as a puppy?
He was ready for IPG 1 at 6 months old.

17. How was he / she like as he / she matured?
A dream to work.

18. How are the dog's litter mates?
Very similar.

19. Is he / she social with other dogs?
Yes.

20. Does the dog live in a house or a kennel?
Both.

Dog 10 - Forny Ze Suutoku Sázavy
(CMKU/BOM/5250/11)

Owner: Jany Böhm

1. How is he / she at home, out of work?

At home Forny is like a quiet lion. He just sleeps in his place in front of our house or in the kennel when it is raining and takes his rest. He is really calm and does not have any stress. Just if somebody is close then 10 metres before our house then he immediately runs and protects the house.

2. Describe his or her character with 5 words..

Dominant, strong, bossy, loyal, original.

3. What is his / her best quality?

The obsession with what he wants and he never gives up. If he decides then he is doing that full power. His passion to work is unbreakable.

4. What is his / her least desirable attribute?

He really doesn't like hot weather but also his aggression from deep inside and very natural. He does never inform you before he does an attack. Just right now and that's it. Nothing before nothing after.

5. Is he / she one of your favourite dogs of all time?

Yes he is the best I ever met.

6. What is his / her favourite activity?

He loves to play with pine cones from a tree and he loves to bite raw bones. Of Course he loves training in general.

7. What is his / her biggest achievements?

Vice Champion FCI 2016 Championship in Slovenia. Winner World cup FMBB 2017 in Germany and World champion of Protection 2016 FCI.

8. Was he / she difficult to train?

He was very difficult on tracking - this took me a long time to find out how to make it best. The rest was quite nice and since the beginning very clear and always full of adrenalin and I like it. Also very funny was to convince him that he must perceive me when he wants something.

9. What's your favourite offspring of his / her?

He has not no offspring. Because he can't be bred. His color is not allowed.

10. How heavy was or is he / she?

He weighs 38 kg.

11. Where is your training club and decoys who helped him / her?

My home club is Suchdol nad Lužnicí - South of czech Republic. My sparring partner was my friend Václav Ouška.

12. If you have the same dog again, what will you so different?

I wouldn't change anything.

13. Is he / she social with people?

Yes he is social. He ignores them and does not search them.

14. Any funny stories you want to share?

After the FCI ceremony I didn't see that he ate the ball I gave him. This is funny now but not back then. We solved it immediately and luckily we did it very well.

15. If you can change 1 thing about the dog, what would it be?

I wouldn't change anything. Because then it wouldn't be him.

16. How was the dog like when he/ she as a puppy?

He was the same, just 30 kg lighter. He since puppy was a character like this. Even at 5 weeks old when I chose him.

17. How was he / she like as he / she matured?

Always the same. When I chose him he was like an adult dog- very sure and very determined to do what he wanted. Then he just grew up physically.

18. How are the dog's litter mates?

He does not have any puppies.

19. Is he / she social with other dogs?

His behaviour is the same as with people. Until no one does anything towards him he just ignores it.

20. Does the dog live in a house or a kennel?

He is living now outside in the garden and he has an open kennel. But whole life when we trained a lot and competed he lived in the kennel. That he is in the garden and free. I promised him my whole life. And now finally he has it.

Dog 11 – Rocky (BRN21071)

Owner: Ray and Stacey Medina

1. How is he / she at home, out of work?

Rocky at home is similar to how he is while working. He is calm and confident.

2. Describe his or her character with 5 words..

Smart, confident, solid, pushy, eager.

3. What is his / her best quality?

Best quality is his willingness to please me. He literally will follow all my commands with or without corrections.

4. What is his / her least desirable attribute?

Least desirable, he is not a social dog. For the most part he only allows my wife and myself to handle him.

5. Is he / she one of your favourite dogs of all time?

Rocky is definitely my favorite dog of all times.

6. What is his / her favourite activity?

His favorite activity is working on a trial field. When he sees the activity he lights up and is ready to go. No hesitation.

7. What is his / her biggest achievements?

Rocky's biggest achievements:

Currently the only living PSA dog with the most legs (Passing score in the level3)

- 2015 PSA3 National Champion
- 2016 PSA3 highest protection score for the year
- 2017 PSA3 Regional Champion
- 2017 PSA3 National Champion
- 2018 PSA3 Regional Champion
- 2019 PSA3 National Champion

8. Was he / she difficult to train?

Rocky was a pleasure to train. Learned very quickly and very eager to please.

9. What's your favourite offspring of his / her?

He was only bred once and I didn't follow the offspring. I was not interested in breeding at that time.

10. How heavy was or is he / she?

Rocky weight is around 75-80lbs

11. Where is your training club and decoys who helped him / her?

I have trained with many talented decoys. To many to list and have participated with many clubs. But in the later years when I was training for the level3 it was with the Jersey Devil Working Dog Club.

12. If you have the same dog again, what will you so different?

If I had the same dog again, I would not do anything differently.

13. Is he / she social with people?

Rocky is definitely not a social dog, but he will ignore everyone and focus on me until I tell him otherwise.

14. Any funny stories you want to share?

One funny story comes to mind. During one of our Thanksgiving meals, Rocky decided he was going to help himself to our finished cook turkey on the table. Needless to say, the entire family had to eat ham as he left nothing for us to eat.

15. If you can change 1 thing about the dog, what would it be?

I would not change anything about this dog. He is now about 12 years old and still has never been sick a day in his life. He still acts like a puppy, but has slowed down quite a bit.

16. How was the dog like when he/ she as a puppy?

I purchased Rocky when he was 15 months old as a green dog. I never knew what he was like as a puppy.

17. How was he / she like as he / she matured?

As a mature dog, he was a hard dog that took corrections well. Eager to please me, but would let me know if my corrections were not fair.

18. How are the dog's litter mates?

Rocky is a VanLeeuwen outcross and the only one of the litter that looked like a Malinois as opposed to the other litter mates that looked like Dutch Shepherds.

19. Is he / she social with other dogs?

He is definitely not social with any other dogs, in fact he is very dominant and aggressive. But with very submissive and passive females (bitches).

20. Does the dog live in a house or a kennel?

He lives in the house in his own "dog room". He is crated when I am not home.

Dog 12 – KP (BRN30573)

Owner: Khoi Pham

1. How is he / she at home, out of work?

KP is great and social out of drive, can be around kids, anybody, cats, but for it is more training because when he was young, if you just looked at him with your eyes, he would go nuts on you, it is in his blood, very high in defense and prey.

2. Describe his or her character with 5 words..

Crazy fuck.

3. What is his / her best quality?

His best quality is drives, tons of drive with high work ethic, his worse quality is also drives, too much drive and sometimes it will leak if I am not on my toes. He is my favorite dog of all time. He just loves to do anything with me, his biggest achievements are completing PSA 2, 2 legs back to back. He is very easy to train because of his drive but also hard to train because of too much drive. He is 24 inches tall and 73 pounds at 3 years old. I have many decoys that help me, Tim Akers, Josh Kirby, Stacey Beller, Darrick Rose.

4. What is his / her least desirable attribute?

If I can change one thing about him, I probably like to control his drive at a younger age, he passed his PSA PDC with zero compulsion training, so this is probably my fault. He is social with other dogs but has to be introduced to them slowly then they can be best friends. I actually use him to teach clients dogs social skill. He is also my retriever for ducks and doves, a protection dog at home, a true working dog. He lives in the house 24/7 free roam, only goes in the crate when we go to training but can also stay in the car when I don't have the crate while other dogs are working.

5. Is he / she one of your favourite dogs of all time?

Don't have too many funny stories about him other than he is a very horny dog, female dogs that got pissed at him for licking their private part gets mad at him and bite but he never bites back.

Dog 13 - Asja (UKC P556-753)

Owner: Greg Williams

1. How is he / she at home, out of work?

Asja was very relaxed around the house. She was just as happy playing catch as she was training for PSA. Very easy dog to live with. Definitely not your typical Malinois.

2. Describe his or her character with 5 words..

Asja in 5 words: smart, driven, loyal, strong character

3. What is his / her best quality?

Best quality: her strong work ethic

4. What is his / her least desirable attribute?

Least favorite attribute: She picked up things a little too quickly. Sometimes it caused conflict in training.

5. Is he / she one of your favourite dogs of all time?

Asja was definitely one of my favorite dogs.

6. What is his / her favourite activity?

Asja's favorite thing was work. Especially bite work.

7. What is his / her biggest achievements?

Asja's biggest achievements: Asja was the last dog to earn her PSA 3 under the old rules when you needed 80% of the points and scenarios were worth more points. She was also inducted into the PSA HoF as the most PSA titled bitch in PSA.

8. Was he / she difficult to train?

Asja was one of those dogs that picked up things easy. If I'm being honest, training with her wasn't really like training. It was just doing. I think what helped is I didn't fall into that sport dog trap, pattern training. In fact, we hardly ever trained for sport. Instead, we focused on training skills and showing her those skills every way we could imagine.

9. What's your favourite offspring of his / her?

My favorite offspring out of Asja never got to see a trial field. It was a pup I named "Hero." I sold him to a friend, who in turn sold him to an elderly woman. I got him back for training at a year old for training and WOW! What an impressive dog. I tried to buy him but she wouldn't sell him. She did eventually sell him to someone in France under the name of "Darth."

10. How heavy was or is he / she?

Asja was between 55-58lbs.

11. Where is your training club and decoys who helped him / her?

Our first club was Capital Cities K-9 in Pasadena, Md. Joe Morris was the club director and the co-founder of PSA.

Joe passed away early in Asja's training. Shortly after I started my own club.

I laid most of her puppy foundation myself. I also had the liberty of having some really awesome decoys in both clubs,

- Darryl Ritchie
- Rick Furrow
- Sean Siggins
- Shawn Edwards
- Charlie Marks
- Josh Stone
- Chad Reynold's
- Lee (last name escapes me).

12. If you have the same dog again, what will you so different?

I'm not really sure I'd do anything different.

13. Is he / she social with people?

Asja was social.

14. Any funny stories you want to share?

I used to take Asja hiking and camping with me. We were hiking in the snow. I was wearing pack boots that I use for late season hunting. We were heading down a steep hill when I suddenly slipped and fell. Asja thought it would be a good idea to go full blown puppy mode (she was 4) and grab me by the boot and drag me another 20 feet to the bottom of the hill. I couldn't get her off because I couldn't stop laughing.

15. If you can change 1 thing about the dog, what would it be?

If I could change one thing about Asja I think I would have wanted her to be a little more serious. She was a prey monster and a little over confident so she really didn't view much as a threat.

16. How was the dog like when he/ she as a puppy?

As a puppy Asja was a typical fun loving, mischievous puppy. Always getting into things, constantly bitting any thing that flapped with a breeze which resulted in much of my clothes being shredded and bleeding arms.

17. How was he / she like as he / she matured?

As Asja matured she seemed to calm down in her house, but lit up like a Christmas tree when she thought she was heading to train or trial. She was like two totally different dogs in that aspect.

18. How are the dog's litter mates?

There were some really nice dogs that came out of her litter. One I remember was a dog named Jaxx owned by Darryl Ritchie. Very hard bitting, solid nerved dog that hit like a train.

19. Is he / she social with other dogs?

Asja was neutral with most dogs. She didn't seek out fights but she didn't hesitate to fight if another dog postured.

20. Does the dog live in a house or a kennel?

Asja was out of Yonas van Joefarm x Rummy van Joe Farm. Yonas was imported from Belgium. Rummy was out of a bitch named Virsla of Naiko Homes who was imported pregnant by Roe van Joe Farm. Here's a link to her pedigree. She was UKC registered.
http://www.pedigreedatabase.com/belgian_malinois/dog.html?id=1785564-asja-van-metro-hoektand

Dog 14 – Cosmo (DN33854601)

Owner: Bob Campanile

1. How is he / she at home, out of work?

When Cosmo is out of work at home, he is still always on the gas. Always looking to do something.

2. Describe his or her character with 5 words..

Intense, loyal, COMMITTED, fearless.

3. What is his / her best quality?

Very trainable.

4. What is his / her least desirable attribute?

Difficult to relax and just turn off.

5. Is he / she one of your favourite dogs of all time?

He is absolutely my favorite work dog out of all my dogs.

6. What is his / her favourite activity?

He enjoys any activity as long as it involves me but overall biting would be his favorite.

7. What is his / her biggest achievements?

Earning his PSA level 3 as well as winning the east coast regional while achieving his first leg in the level 3. Earning the high level 2 score for the year. National vice champion level 3.

8. Was he / she difficult to train?

Cosmo was one of the easiest dogs for me to train. The difficulty occurred only through my error.

9. What's your favourite offspring of his / her?

Cosmo has only fathered 1 litter and I lost contact with all but one pup.

10. How heavy was or is he / she?

He is small about 58 lbs

11. Where is your training club and decoys who helped him / her?

It is my club, Jersey Devil Working Dog Club located here in NJ at my home. Many decoys at our club are responsible for our success. Ray Medina, Andrew Gellagos, Mike Fraas, EJ Parker.

12. If you have the same dog again, what will you so different?

Teach him to relax and collect himself before getting what he wants.

13. Is he / she social with people?

He is super social and absolutely loves people and dogs.

14. Any funny stories you want to share?

Funny now but not when it happened. Training one time he literally ran head first into a heavy wooden meter jump. Never jumped over it, he went right through it. Never skipped a beat and didn't slow down the least bit. Did injure his front shoulder and leg but not seriously. Not funny at the time but looking back at it now very funny.

15. If you can change 1 thing about the dog, what would it be?

Just being able to calm down a bit easier.

16. How was the dog like when he/ she as a puppy?

He was absolutely the best puppy in the world. I wouldn't change a thing about his puppy time. I was truly spoiled by this puppy/dog.

17. How was he / she like as he / she matured?

Again, even while maturing into adulthood he continued to amaze me. I couldn't ask for anything better.

18. How are the dog's litter mates?

I have no knowledge of any of his litter mates other than one female that was basically a pet/demo type dog.

19. Is he / she social with other dogs?

Very social with dogs

20. Does the dog live in a house or a kennel?

During his working career he was crated. Since retiring he's shares his time crated and in the house with my family and I.

Dog 15 - Lite vom Adlerauge
(VDH/DMC11/0311malin1873/H/13)

Owner: Arnold Kivágó

1. How is he / she at home, out of work?

He loves sleeping on the sofa and hanging around in the garden.

2. Describe his or her character with 5 words..

Social, active, dominant with the helper, hard worker, balanced in drives.

3. What is his / her best quality?

His super willingness for work.

4. What is his / her least desirable attribute?

I can not name anything, he is perfect for me.

5. Is he / she one of your favourite dogs of all time?

Absolutely.

6. What is his / her favourite activity?

Protection work.

7. What is his / her biggest achievements?

FMBB world champion.

8. Was he / she difficult to train?

No.

9. What's your favourite offspring of his / her?

Sadly he does not have many offspring.

10. How heavy was or is he / she?

31kg

11. Where is your training club and decoys who helped him / her?

We train in Mogyoród,Hungary,the town where I live. His helpers were Dajka József, Studinher Ferenc, Serhokk Gábor, Zok Péter, Rácz Attila, He achieved his biggest trial results with József and Ferenc.

12. If you have the same dog again, what will you so different?

Totally different, probably nothing. I would do little changes in obedience and tracking.

13. Is he / she social with people?

Yes,he is very clear in head, no problems with other people.

14. Any funny stories you want to share?

I always loved the way he started the bark and hold like a beagle. If he is very angry, he makes it 2 times. Every time

I was competing with him he made so happy minutes to the audience with this special style.

15. If you can change 1 thing about the dog, what would it be?

To have more offspring from him.

16. How was the dog like when he/ she as a puppy?

Open, friendly puppy who was very active. Loved to eat, loved to play, loved to work. He was a fantastic partner in the training.

17. How was he / she like as he / she matured?

17. How was he / she like as he / she matured?

He kept all his good abilities that he had as a puppy.And plus he gave super force to the grips,good dominance on the helper, all the positive stuff that maturing can add to a good young dog.

18. How are the dog's litter mates?

I don't know too much about the littermates.

19. Is he / she social with other dogs?

Yes, he is social. But I don't let him hang with other adult male dogs. He is not starting a fight, but he would finish it.

20. Does the dog live in a house or a kennel?

He lives in the house as a pet, with the family.

Dog 16 - Edden aka torky (LOSH977755)

Owner: Christoph Joris

1. How is he / she at home, out of work?

Out of work Edden was a very calm dog.

2. Describe his or her character with 5 words..

Stability,self confident, honest, strong, dominant

3. What is his / her best quality?

A power grip

4. What is his / her least desirable attribute?

The out

5. Is he / she one of your favourite dogs of all time?

Yes one of my favourite ones.

6. What is his / her favourite activity?

Bitework

7. What is his / her biggest achievements?

Being the father of champions in different federations.

8. Was he / she difficult to train?

Yes

9. What's your favourite offspring of his / her?

K'Lasco

10. How heavy was or is he / she?

40 kg

11. Where is your training club and decoys who helped him / her?

My club is DTC Ghoy in Belgium

12. If you have the same dog again, what will you so different?

Nothing

13. Is he / she social with people?

He was very social

14. Any funny stories you want to share?

Many decoys call him the BONEBREAKER.

15. If you can change 1 thing about the dog, what would it be?

Perfect like he was.

16. How was the dog like when he/ she as a puppy?

Came to me when he was an adult.

17. How was he / she like as he / she matured?

Strong in every meaning of the word.

18. How are the dog's litter mates?

Don't know.

19. Is he / she social with other dogs?

Yes he was.

20. Does the dog live in a house or a kennel?

Part in the house, part in the kennel.

So, I met Christoph in 2005 when I first immigrated to Belgium in pursuit of my dog sport career. But it was 2009 that we started training together. By that time Torky was in his prime and he was about three years. One of the first things that Christoph wanted me to do in the club was to give Torky a bite, not to train him, but to let me appreciate the power of the dog. What I can tell you. The grip of this dog was unbelievable. His strength alone already puts you in awe. But it was also his attitude in the bite, the bad intention. When you're in the suit for him, you know he's not playing. It's not a game for him. When he puts his teeth around your shin, his goal is to drill you and break you. I mean, Torky was a social and fair dog. Christoph had given me the leash to take him for a walk. The dog would just stroll along, minding his own business like you don't exist. But when he bites, he goes into a different mode.

Out of work, Torky was cool and aloof. He was not the type of dog that cared for a pat from his owner or begging for attention. He was content living in his own world and doing his own things, unless you want to offer him a bite, then he was always up for it. He had a calm and collected demeanour. He was aloof but he was also clear in the head. If a stranger approached him and acted friendly and fair, he would show no aggression. With puppies he was super, very gentle and friendly with them. When he looked at you, you could feel his presence. He had this kind of piercing focus that can burn a hole in you. I think the word Alpha dog has been over used in the dog world. I don't believe there are many true Alphas. Just because a dog shows some dominance doesn't necessarily mean he is an Alpha. However, for me Torky was truly an Alpha dog. He had all the characteristics of an Alpha, stability, strength, focus, fairness, composure, presence, hardness and rank. On top of these, he produced his qualities. Look at the success his progeny have in various bite sports. Christoph has had a lot of special dogs over the years, but Torky was one of a kind.

EDDEN
LOSH 977755 (JORIS)
(C)2012 VIKTORIA FAZIKAS - WWW.ANIMEDIA24.DE

Dog 17 - A'Tim (NVBK16241)

Owner: Martine Joâo Lopes

A'Tim was 'the complete package'. Very charismatic dog with an extremely strong personality. Very dominant alpha type of dog and very devoted to his family.

Strong athletic body and genetic working quality.

Deep, genetic grips and a very clear head.

No unnecessary aggressive attitude. He didn't need that to impress. He radiated confidence and natural dominance that made everyone respect him.

A natural 'don't mess with me' attitude without being aggressive.

1. How is he / she at home, out of work?

At home he was a very cool dog.

Not nervous at all. Very nice dog to have around in the house.

2. Describe his or her character with 5 words..

Charismatic, confident, dominant, driven, loyal

3. What is his / her best quality?

Natural dominance, fearless

4. What is his / her least desirable attribute?

Needed a very strong handler (then again, I wouldn't exactly call this undesirable)

5. Is he / she one of your favourite dogs of all time?

Definitely! He was the foundation dog of a very strong bloodline.

6. What is his / her favourite activity?

He loved to work!

Whether it was obedience, jumping, retrieving or bitework, he did everything with the same intensity

7. What is his / her biggest achievements?

Even though he wasn't exactly a sporty type of dog (he was very 'serious'), he achieved many victories and titles. The most important ones:
- National Champion NVBK Cat1 (highest level)
- Grand Prix Winner
- DMC Körung 3

8. Was he / she difficult to train?

He needed a very strong and experienced handler and an experienced team to assist.

Could be very dangerous when provoked.

Joâo Lopes is kind of a 'human A'Tim version' so they fit together very well.

9. What's your favourite offspring of his / her?

We have several generations of dogs that really take after him.

"Quality prevails, generation after generation"

https://workingmalinois3.wixsite.com/workingmalinois/mission
www.workingmalinois.be

He has top notch offspring all over the world. Not only in sports, but numerous also are working the streets as Police K9's and in the military and Special Forces units

2019 World Champions Mondioring 2 and 3 + Bronze Medal all have him in their bloodline.

National Champions Belgian Ring 2018 and 2019 are offspring.

Several National Champions IPO in different countries.

Our boy Fun du Bois de la Limite National Champion NVBK 2011 and his son Ringstar F-Kuno one of the most famous Malinois of the last decade

Quite a few offspring in the the World Championships IPO in the last decade

I could go on and on and still forget to mention many.

10. How heavy was or is he / she?

34kg and 64cm at the shoulder

11. Where is your training club and decoys who helped him / her?

He was trained at the famous nvbk club of Hoboken Vinkevelden.

Decoys were Bart Bellon, Dirk Nauwelaerts and Timothy Rotsaert.

The last 2 years of his career, we trained in Lummen with decoy Dirk Swerten.

12. If you have the same dog again, what will you so different?

I guess we'd do exactly the same

13. Is he / she social with people?

He was very devoted to his own family. Would have given his life to protect us.

He didn't like strangers but would leave them alone as long as he wasn't provoked.

14. Any funny stories you want to share?

For the Körung 3 test, there was a real life scenario, where there would be a civil attack, out of the blue and off the field, to test the dog's courage.

We were doing such a scenario in the forest a few days before and there were a few people from abroad, who were visiting us to join some training.

I told them to stay behind me and not to move when Joâo and Tim came closer, because they were going to be attacked and things could get rough. The dog would know that it was a serious situation and he would get very serious himself.

So when the attack took place, it did get rough indeed.

I was concentrating on what was happening and didn't pay attention to my visitors and when I looked back afterwards, they were up in a tree!

15. If you can change 1 thing about the dog, what would it be?

I would make him immortal so we'd be together forever

16. How was the dog like when he/ she as a puppy?

We didn't have him as a pup, but from what we heard he was quite a wild one.

We bought him as an 18 months old dog. He was too much for his previous owner and the guy was afraid of him.

17. How was he / she like as he / she matured?

He still was pretty wild and it took a lot of experience to get control over him and compete top level

18. How are the dog's litter mates?

We knew only one litter sister and she was a very nice and confident female. She wasn't trained.

19. Is he / she social with other dogs?

He was ok with other dogs as long as they didn't provoke him.

I always took him on hikes with his son Fils and he was great with puppies too

20. Does the dog live in a house or a kennel?

When Joâo was home, he lived in a kennel outdoors.

But when I was home alone (my husband often worked night shifts), he lived with me in the house. The perfect bodyguard!

Dog 18 - Jerry Vom Zabelstein
(N.H.S.B.NR.VDH/DMC11/0326)

Owner: Sandy Lips

1. How is he / she at home, out of work?

When he is at home with me, he is relaxed but always one eye open!

2. Describe his or her character with 5 words..

His character :

Loyal

Powerfull

Self assured

Workmaniac

Strong

3. What is his / her best quality?

His best quality is that he is always ready to work, no matter what time, day or place... Bring it on!

4. What is his / her least desirable attribute?

He does not like cats!!

5. Is he / she one of your favourite dogs of all time?

Yes he is my favorite dog of all time!

He has a special place in my heart.

6. What is his / her favourite activity?

His favorite activity is almost everything that has something to do with being active. Like.. Biking, on the treadmill, swimming, hiking. But the ultimate thing for him is protection work!! He loves it!

7. What is his / her biggest achievements?

In 2015. 2th place Dutch Championship.

In 2016. 18th place on FMBB World Cup

In 2016. 1th place vdh coenstad.

In 2017. 1th place Dutch Championship

In 2017. 3th place FMBB World Cup

In 2017. 3th place Final of the FMBB

In 2018. 3th place nbg Midden Brabant

In 2018. 5th place Dutch Championship all breeds.

In 2019. 4th place nationals.

In 2019. 2th place nbg Brabant bokaal.

8. Was he / she difficult to train?

In the beginning he was not always easy to train, but the more we got to know each other the more we became a team!

10. How heavy was or is he / she?

His weight was during full power training between 33-35 kilo.

11. Where is your training club and decoys who helped him / her?

My training was in Spijkenisse at VDH club " De Oude Maas" en K9 Center Ysselsteyn.

12. If you have the same dog again, what will you so different?

The decoy who helped me were Robbie de Jong and Tobias Oleynik.

13. Is he / she social with people?

I would not change a thing!

14. Any funny stories you want to share?

He is not social with all people, just a few.

15. If you can change 1 thing about the dog, what would it be?

Again I would not change a thing!

16. How was the dog like when he/ she as a puppy?

He was a funny puppy, chasing cars and bicycles, rabbits, anything that had a little bit of speed he chased.

17. How was he / she like as he / she matured?

He became very stable when he matured but every now and then he tried something he never did before. Also on trials.

18. How are the dog's litter mates?

The litter mates I do not know so much about. They are all in different countries.

19. Is he / she social with other dogs?

Jerry vom Zabel stein is very social with females and puppies. He loves them.

But other males he does not have a connection with.

20. Does the dog live in a house or a kennel?

When I was training Jerry vom Zabelstein he lived in a kennel. This he loved.

But now since he enjoys his retirement he stays in the house a lot. Also during the night. He earned it!

He has proven himself so many times and even now when he is not in the full training program, he is still ready to go!

This is why I love Jerry so much, ready to work for me and protects me at all times!

There is no other dog like Jerry Vom Zabelstein.

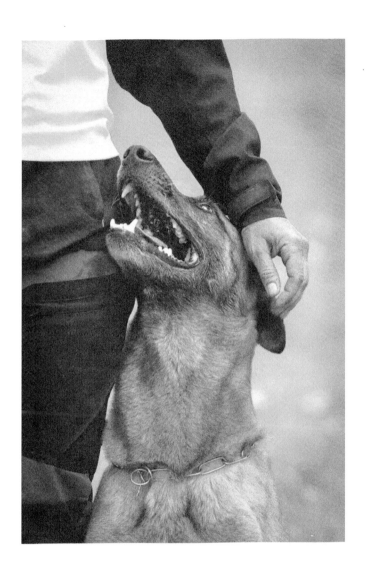

Dog 19 – Bowie (BRN24640)

Owner: Arjen Heuten

1. How is he / she at home, out of work?

At home he is a friendly dog , to children and animals.

2. Describe his or her character with 5 words..

Stubborn, kind, hard, reliable.

3. What is his / her best quality?

His grip, he does anything for the bite.

4. What is his / her least desirable attribute?

Ball.

5. Is he / she one of your favourite dogs of all time?

No that was Barry, my other dog was my all time favorite.

6. What is his / her favourite activity?

Work on the field, biting, jumping on everything. A dog that loves all actions regarding working.

7. What is his / her biggest achievements?

PH1

8. Was he / she difficult to train?

Yes very difficult , he was a stubborn dog from when he was a puppy.

9. What's your favourite offspring of his / her?

Non special.

10. How heavy was or is he / she?

38 kilo

11. Where is your training club and decoys who helped him / her?

I train at my own club PHV Enter and in Enter NL with different decoys.

12. If you have the same dog again, what will you so different?

I would sell the dog, it's not much fun to train a dog like that, with such behavior and mentality.

13. Is he / she social with people?

Yes he is very social.

14. Any funny stories you want to share?

It's funny when you push him or tease him, then he would tear a bush out off the ground with roots and all.

15. If you can change 1 thing about the dog, what would it be?

His stubbornness and hard headedness.

16. How was the dog like when he/ she as a puppy?

Crazy like hell, you could hang him on a key in the door and he would hold on to it for as long as he could, he would bite hoses and anything he came across.

17. How was he / she like as he / she matured?

He is now more conversational and kinder than when he was a puppy.

18. How are the dog's litter mates?

I don't know.

19. Is he / she social with other dogs?

Yes he is social with other dogs.

20. Does the dog live in a house or a kennel?

He lives in a kennel.

Dog 20 - Parendo vinces cordell Walker
(LOSH948823 / AKC DN24843401)

Owner: Erdinç Sarimusaoğlu

1. How is he / she at home, out of work?

He is kind of a dog who can spend time alone. So at home he is calm and living with him is easy.

2. Describe his or her character with 5 words..

He is a self-sufficient, workaholic, confident, cold-blooded (not hectic) dog with high drives.

3. What is his / her best quality?

Bite work. Calm and hard offensive grips.

4. What is his / her least desirable attribute?

He can be such a hard dog when mating. So, mating can be sometimes quite risky when doing with a newbie bitch. He doesn't like to be touched when there is a girl in heat.

5. Is he / she one of your favourite dogs of all time?

Yes he is. Not only because of his achievements in competitions, but because of him being himself.

6. What is his / her favourite activity?

For sure first mating and bitework other than that he likes to fetch frisbee, especially in the sea.

7. What is his / her biggest achievements?

In 2017 FMBB WC, he made the 7th place in total points and 3rd place in protection as the youngest dog of the championship. He was only 2.5 years old and first time in a big championship.

8. Was he / she difficult to train?

As a puppy it was difficult to motivate the dog for obedience.

9. What's your favourite offspring of his / her?

Males: DJ Red Phoenix(Asia Red Phoenix*Parendo Vinces Cordell Walker)

Ivan Red Phoenix (Asia Red Phoenix*Parendo Vinces Cordell Walker)

Ares (B'Joy Lobo Grande* Parendo Vinces Cordell Walker)

Females: Electra V. Assy Krum (Berta Red Phoenix* Parendo Vinces Cordell Walker)

10. How heavy was or is he / she?

38kg

11. Where is your training club and decoys who helped him / her?

Istanbul-Club Von Juliet, Friedrichshafen Hundeplatz. My helpers are in Friedrichshafen, Yener Yüksel and Oliver Neubrand.

12. If you have the same dog again, what will you so different?

If I didn't have to drive 2400 kms to train with a helper, that would be nice. So that we would have more time to train for protection.

13. Is he / she social with people?

He will tolerate people he knows but not very social with people. He is a cool dog.

14. Any funny stories you want to share?

When he was young, I used to train heeling before mating and before releasing him for sex, I would use 'ok' command. On his first IPO trial, as we were heeling, the judge decided to start the routine all over again because there was no gun shot. He stopped me and told me this and I said 'ok'. And Kaiser(my dog) directly ran to the male dog on a down stay under distraction exercise and started humping him. It was a really hard time for me and the other dog.

15. If you can change 1 thing about the dog, what would it be?

There is nothing I would like to change about him.

16. How was the dog like when he/ she as a puppy?

He was a cool puppy who could spend 5 hours with only a ball alone.

17. How was he / she like as he / she matured?

He was the same stable dog from puppyhood until now. Not much changed with him and that is a quality I would go for.

18. How are the dog's litter mates?

A brother of him attended in FCI and FMBB WCs. He made 28th place.

19. Is he / she social with other dogs?

He is ok.

20. Does the dog live in a house or a kennel?

He lives in the house.

Dog 21 - Jonny de la Montagne Unique
(0HZBMAL12973)

Owner: Cornelia Hämmerle

1. How is he / she at home, out of work?

Out of work he is in the kennel or in our big field who is closed with a fence.

2. Describe his or her character with 5 words..

Self confident, really a lot of prey drive, social to people and other dogs, and very hard to himself

3. What is his / her best quality?

His prey drive and his hardness

4. What is his / her least desirable attribute?

He likes to destroy all at home

5. Is he / she one of your favourite dogs of all time?

Jonny teached me a lot, I love him!

6. What is his / her favourite activity?

Destroy something or training!

Also walking and running on the treadmill

7. What is his / her biggest achievements?

To learn everything by the age of five and get the 10th place at FMBB 2017.

8. Was he / she difficult to train?

His will to please is less, his hardness and his own head big.

9. What's your favourite offspring of his / her?

There are a lot, Jonny mated late, the puppies are coming soon.

10. How heavy was or is he / she?

32 kg

11. Where is your training club and decoys who helped him / her?

The first 4 years we trained with his breeder, there was no future so I stopped training for 1 year! Then I thought we need a second chance, I want to hear from Peter Scherk if it's possible to make better competitions with Jonny! Then the new way of training started - Peter and Connie Scherk, their training made it possible.

12. If you have the same dog again, what will you so different?

Training like Heuwinkl Style from the beginning.

13. Is he / she social with people?

Yes.

14. Any funny stories you want to share?

No.

15. If you can change 1 thing about the dog, what would it be?

More will to please.

16. How was the dog like when he/ she as a puppy?

Very easy puppy, he slept well from the beginning, was self confident and open.

17. How was he / she like as he / she matured?

The same.

18. How are the dog's litter mates?

Jonny has 1 brother, the owner didn't make dogsport.

19. Is he / she social with other dogs?

Yes.

20. Does the dog live in a house or a kennel?

In an indoor kennel.

Dog 22 – Brodie

Owner: Danny Wells

1. How is he / she at home, out of work?

Brodie was really relaxed at home. Able to switch off and be a pet. Done a number of home invasion scenarios and he switched on instantly.

2. Describe his or her character with 5 words..

Bold, friendly, courageous, driven and brave.

3. What is his / her best quality?

Brodie's best quality was how serious he was whilst being under complete control, regardless of the environment. He also has extremely low self preservation when in a fight.

4. What is his / her least desirable attribute?

His least favourite attribute would be his elements of his environmentals. He grew up on a farm in the middle of nowhere so he never had a great environmental start. I was playing catch up with this.

5. Is he / she one of your favourite dogs of all time?

Brodie is without a doubt, my favourite dog of all time. He was just that one dog to me.

6. What is his / her favourite activity?

Favourite activity was chase and attacks. Especially bike attack scenarios.

7. What is his / her biggest achievements?

Brodie's biggest achievements are winning Lorockmor level 3 twice, back to back. First time, there were 23 dogs. Second time, there were 17 dogs.

8. Was he / she difficult to train?

Brodie was a little difficult at the start but once he'd bonded me he was great to train.

9. What's your favourite offspring of his / her?

Brodie has no offsprings.

10. How heavy was or is he / she?

40kg.

11. Where is your training club and decoys who helped him / her?

My training club is based in St. Helens. Jay Lowe helped decoy for Brodie. We were working together back then.

12. If you have the same dog again, what will you so different?

If I had Brodie again (hopefully from a pup) I'd blast his environmentals.

13. Is he / she social with people?

Very social with people. I used to do demos with him all over the country. He'd go from bite scenarios to getting pictures with kids in a flash.

14. Any funny stories you want to share?

When I first got Brodie, I was once on a site working with my other dog. I got Brodie out for some much needed environmentals when all of a sudden a loud crash was heard (forklift dropped a pallet) Brodie went to bolt and when he realised he was on lead, he flew at me! I have a full blown fight with him in front of about 12 workmen, who were mortified. I got the dog under manners, looked at the fellas and said "evening chaps" then just walked off.

15. If you can change 1 thing about the dog, what would it be?

I wouldn't have changed anything, you know. He could have had better environmentals but I'd say that was just a lack of exposure from a young age.

16. How was the dog like when he/ she as a puppy?

Unfortunately, I never saw him as a puppy but I was told he was a right handful. Which is why he was sold to me.

17. How was he / she like as he / she matured?

Just a solid all round dog. Got harder as he matured but more level headed.

18. How are the dog's litter mates?

A mix! Some were passed about for being too much dog but I know of one that has been with the same handler his whole life. All solid dogs though. They all work.

19. Is he / she social with other dogs?

Brodie was social with other dogs but he was very assertive. Any disorder and he would want to dish out lessons. To this day, I've not had another dog that had such influence on other dogs. I put that down to spending the first 14 months of his life living outside with 12 or so other adult dogs.

20. Does the dog live in a house or a kennel?

Brodie lived in the house with me. But he could settle anywhere.

Dog 23 - Dackx Perle de Tourbière (BRN7773)

Owner: Yvonne and Jan Timmermans

1. How is he / she at home, out of work?

Easy at home and crazy at work.

2. Describe his or her character with 5 words..

Friendly, powerful, fearless, unstoppable, 100% fair.

3. What is his / her best quality?

His powerful drive for work always.

4. What is his / her least desirable attribute?

Really, he did not have one.

5. Is he / she one of your favourite dogs of all time?

Absolutely.

6. What is his / her favourite activity?

He loved everything.

7. What is his / her biggest achievements?

His breeding career with proven results and of course PH I 419 CL And a competition: 5-kringen Limburg 2009: 2nd place 427 points

8. Was he / she difficult to train?

Yes he was, because of his extreme drives.

9. What's your favourite offspring of his / her?

There are so many but I think our Keurras van het Groot wezenland, he was almost a clone of Dackx in everything.

10. How heavy was or is he / she?

I think about 35 kilos.

11. Where is your training club and decoys who helped him / her?

We trained in The Netherlands with Jan Tinnemans (also good friend) for many many years, Our decoys are Huub Timmermans (also owner of Dackx) and Peter Neijnens and since some years Ron Dirkx.

12. If you have the same dog again, what will you so different?

Nothing.

13. Is he / she social with people?

Very social.

14. Any funny stories you want to share?

He loves to jump in the water from an old cargo ship.

15. If you can change 1 thing about the dog, what would it be?

Make him alive again.

16. How was the dog like when he/ she as a puppy?

As a puppy he was already eager for work.

17. How was he / she like as he / she matured?

Friend, powerful, fearless, unstoppable, 100% fair

18. How are the dog's litter mates?

Similarly a famous one is Dylan Perle de Tourbière.

19. Is he / she social with other dogs?

Yes always been, just the last few years when he became older, he prefered to be left alone by other dogs. Puppies he always loved!

20. Does the dog live in a house or a kennel?

Dackx always lived in a kennel.

Dog 24 – Tourtel (NVBK13075)

Owner: Luc Josten

1. How is he / she at home, out of work?

At home, the dog was watchful and quiet. He was in a kennel outside and never came in the house.

2. Describe his or her character with 5 words..

Smart, strong, watchful, fair and agile.

3. What is his / her best quality?

He always wanted to work for his boss.

4. What is his / her least desirable attribute?

He has no bad qualities.

5. Is he / she one of your favourite dogs of all time?

Yes, he was the best I ever had!

6. What is his / her favourite activity?

When he has to bite the decoy.

7. What is his / her biggest achievements?

Champion of Belgium 1996 and Champion of the big prize of the provinces 1997.

8. Was he / she difficult to train?

No, he always wanted to train.

9. What's your favourite offspring of his / her?

The dog named Enig.

10. How heavy was or is he / she?

34 kg

11. Where is your training club and decoys who helped him / her?

De Verdedigingshond Beerse

Decoys: Sooi Van Steenbergen and Peter Schellekens

12. If you have the same dog again, what will you so different?

I Will try to do the same.

13. Is he / she social with people?

No, he was fair to us but not to strangers.

14. Any funny stories you want to share?

When he participated in a game, the opponents were not happy with it. They laughed about it and said they were playing for second place.

15. If you can change 1 thing about the dog, what would it be?

Nothing

16. How was the dog like when he/ she as a puppy?

Fair, free, playful

17. How was he / she like as he / she matured?

Confident

18. How are the dog's litter mates?

His brother also played for years in the NVBK.

19. Is he / she social with other dogs?

Very social

20. Does the dog live in a house or a kennel?

He lived in a kennel.

Dog 25 - Pep van de Suikerdijk (23956 NVBK BR)

Owner: Nadia van overloop

On 04/05/2012 the litter was born out of the combination Nessy NVBK (daughter of F'Randy & Kelsey) & Edden (Torky LOSH).

4 males & 5 females.

3 puppies from that litter we kept Pio, Pep & Pippa, 2 brothers and a sister.

The training could start NVBK ring sport with us at the club in Zwijndrecht & with Joris Christoph in Goy, top training. The puppies were very promising so the result was inevitable.

At the age of less than 3 years in March 2015 their first game, which followed were several good results with first places.

Result all three dogs selected for the National Championship cat 3 in September 2015 including Pio van de Suikerdijk best classified and Pep 3rd classified.

A beautiful day with Pep, 1st Belgium camp as the end result. Pippa 2nd and Pio 3rd, never has anyone achieved that in the NVBK. In the same year Pio also became champion of the Province of Antwerp.

In 2016 all three dogs were again selected for the championship cat 2 Pio again best classified with the end result and Pep 1st place from Belgium then Pio 2nd and Pippa 4th place.

They are all three dogs with a strong character and a high work drive and very good jumpers, but at home quiet & friendly dogs should be like a good working dog.

In 2019, unfortunately, the career of Pio came to an end due to injury to the buttock muscle.

Pio Van de Suikerdijk NVBK 23957

National camp. best classified in

2015 - 2016 & 2017

prov.camp. Antwerp 2015

GPDP winner in 2017-2018 & 2019.

National camp. cat 1 in 2018

Pep Van de Suikerdijk NVBK 23956

Wet. camp. cat 3 2015

Wet. camp. cat 2 2016

prov.camp. Antwerp 2018

winner Duel der kamp. 2017 This is a competition among the champions of every cat and province in the past year.

Pippa van de suikerdijk is a top bitch who has given us and many other good offspring including our Troy Van de Suikerdijk, son of Pippa Van de Suikerdijk & Jacky van't Randgeval.

Troy has already proven his qualities as a stud dog several times with very good offspring in sports and with the police at home and abroad, good genes do not lie.

Pep Van de Suikerdijk

1. How is he / she at home, out of work?

Very quiet yet watchful.

2. Describe his or her character with 5 words..

Strong, confident, stable, friendly and alert.

3. What is his / her best quality?

Guarding the object.

4. What is his / her least desirable attribute?

Unloading at the bite work.

5. Is he / she one of your favourite dogs of all time?

Very sure

6. What is his / her favourite activity?

The bite work he loves.

7. What is his / her biggest achievements?

N/A

8. Was he / she difficult to train?

No

9. What's your favourite offspring of his / her?

no offspring

10. How heavy was or is he / she?

38 kg

11. Where is your training club and decoys who helped him / her?

Zwijndrecht (Belgium) & DTC Ghoy with Joris Christoph.

12. If you have the same dog again, what will you so different?

Nothing has always been well worked on the dog.

13. Is he / she social with people?

Yes

14. Any funny stories you want to share?

N/A

15. If you can change 1 thing about the dog, what would it be?

Maybe a fuller bite.

16. How was the dog like when he/ she as a puppy?

Cheerful and stable always in for play and work.

17. How was he / she like as he / she matured?

Strong confident dog that will never let you down.

18. How are the dog's litter mates?

Most are on the same line.

19. Is he / she social with other dogs?

Yes, but best with dogs he knows.

20. Does the dog live in a house or a kennel?

In a kennel.

Pep van de suikerdijk

White number 7.   2015 Belgium champion cat 3.   2016 Belgium champion cat 2.   Champion province Antwerpen 2017 & winner Duel der Champions 2018.

Dog 26 - Ferro du Mont St. Aubert (23957 NVBK BR)

Owner: Marc-Oliver Radke

1. How is he / she at home, out of work?

He is an absolutely calm dog at home.

2. Describe his or her character with 5 words..

Dominant, good natural balanced aggression, self confident, hardness, high will to work.

3. What is his / her best quality?

The ability to work on the highest level of ipo sport and also as police protection and narcotic dog for long years and as police dog even today.

4. What is his / her least desirable attribute?

Food aggression.

5. Is he / she one of your favourite dogs of all time?

Absolutely.

6. What is his / her favourite activity?

Every kind of work.

7. What is his / her biggest achievements?

Many many good jobs he did at police work. In sport 6th place on FMBB WC. But sport is not my most important thing.

8. Was he / she difficult to train?

Yes, we had a lot of problems with his dominance in the beginning. And later with the high motivation he has.

9. What's your favourite offspring of his / her?

For me it is Quick vom Gsiberger.

10. How heavy was or is he / she?

32 kg.

11. Where is your training club and decoys who helped him / her?

We train in a small group in the south of Germany without a club. The decoys who helped me a lot were Markus Neutz in the beginning, and mainly Heinz Huonker and Jörg Schwabe and at the end of his career Oliver Schilling

12. If you have the same dog again, what will you so different?

I can't say it was easy. I think I would do the tracking in a different way.

13. Is he / she social with people?

Because of his work, not really.

14. Any funny stories you want to share?

No.

15. If you can change 1 thing about the dog, what would it be?

The food aggression

16. How was the dog like when he/ she as a puppy?

He was very active from the beginning. Stable and self confident with high dominance.

17. How was he / she like as he / she matured?

Similar.

18. How are the dog's litter mates?

I can not understand the question. you mean the females?

19. Is he / she social with other dogs?

Yes he is.

20. Does the dog live in a house or a kennel?

Both but mainly in the kennel.

Dog 27 – Harold (BRN26214)

Owner: Kitty Van Driel

I bought Harold as a puppy and picked him up when he was eight weeks old. All he did in the beginning was sleep and grow. On the training field he was often very present. His behavior as a young dog was curious. He was a very free puppy who has never shown any fear in any strange situation. Because he grew so fast I only trained with him the first year the exercises that did not burden his physical condition. As a puppy of 3 months old I let Harold go into the woods independently to find the box and man. Harold controlled both exercises when he was 4 months young. His fetching was also very good. As a puppy he kept looking for a tube and remained very concentrated in this. Because he kept growing fast for a long time he was a bit lanky so running fast was a bit of a problem for him. Because of that I waited longer to send him out of the lane. When he was a year he had a height of 28 inch.

When he was one year old we started biting. With a year and a half I was able to send Harold for 32 feet. Shortly after we started the biting with him I had to shut down Harold again, because I had to bring another dog to trial. After the trial I switched club and started training with Harold again. I then immediately started sending him on full distance. Harold established but did not yet have the attack like he has now. I started calling back and the rest of the set of exercises. Harold had a chase problem for three months lucky enough he solved the problem itself. Because I put in his training until now a lot of pressure, Harold now has solid nerves and is stable in all exercises. The fake attack was a bit difficult to learn. But within six months, I had Harold ready in the entire program and did a trial to see what his level was; we finished fourth. After this I visited a lot of clubs with various decoys and in different areas. Harold grew on his behavior each training. His work ethic and willingness to train are great. He hardly misses any object in the tracking and trailing. Because of the good base and because he is a hard and strong dog also in mind, other exercises and programs can still be learned easily. Harold keeps going and continues to work for me. You can reward Harold in the program after a practice with a tube or ball. Once the helper is on the field, he no longer cares about other things and only sees the helper as a reward. Harold only has one boss he listens to. Another can train with him, but then Harold does what he feels like.

We also trained Harold in a number of civil situations. Here again you see the down-to-earth courageous dog coming forward again. It is a super dog both in the various KNPV programs and in citizen actions in buildings. Harold is a hard and strong dog with solid nerves. I now have an offspring. He, too, is already at full distance at 20 weeks in the woods and bites the suit very well.

Harold is calm at home. He can lie in the house but this has a negative effect on his training. As soon as Harold is in the house for a week, listening in training decreases. He is social towards children and his environment, but is very watchful and certainly at home in charge of my pack. Towards other dogs he is sociable until a certain level. You have to keep working him because otherwise he will start to show demolition behavior.

If I have to briefly describe Harold's character:

It is a very down to earth and courageous dog and very boss oriented. He likes to work and learn things. The revier, bite and retrieve drives are amply present.

Dog 28 - Pio van de suikerdijk (23957 NVBK BR)

Owner: Marc Oste

1. How is he / she at home, out of work?

Very quiet yet watchful.

2. Describe his or her character with 5 words..

Stable, confident, strong, alert and friendly to his own people.

3. What is his / her best quality?

Full grip.

4. What is his / her least desirable attribute?

Difficult to loose in transport.

5. Is he / she one of your favourite dogs of all time?

Very sure.

6. What is his / her favourite activity?

Bite work he likes that.

7. What is his / her biggest achievements?

3 times winner of the grand prize of the province. Champion of Belgium cat 1 in 2018 and champion of Antwerp 2015.

8. Was he / she difficult to train?

In some exercises.

9. What's your favourite offspring of his / her?

Has offspring but not known.

10. How heavy was or is he / she?

40 kg.

11. Where is your training club and decoys who helped him / her?

Zwijndrecht (Belgium) + DTC Ghoy with Joris Christoph and decoy Sven Pultyn.

12. If you have the same dog again, what will you so different?

More stable in the transport.

13. Is he / she social with people?

Yes now, not before.

14. Any funny stories you want to share?

N/A.

15. If you can change 1 thing about the dog, what would it be?

Slightly more stable in its early years.

16. How was the dog like when he/ she as a puppy?

Always in for work and play, slightly more reserved against strangers.

17. How was he / she like as he / she matured?

Strong powerful dog.

18. How are the dog's litter mates?

Most are on the same line.

19. Is he / she social with other dogs?

No, only with dogs from our kennel.

20. Does the dog live in a house or a kennel?

In a kennel but can also enter the house.

Dog 29 - Pippa Van De Suikerdijk (23960 NVBK BR)

Owner: Nadia Van Overloop

1. How is he / she at home, out of work?

Quietly alert at the right time.

2. Describe his or her character with 5 words..

Friendly, alert, stable, confident and a good mother for her puppies.

3. What is his / her best quality?

Guarding the object.

4. What is his / her least desirable attribute?

Bite at the interrupted.

5. Is he / she one of your favourite dogs of all time?

You will not find a better bitch.

6. What is his / her favourite activity?

Weeks in the field.

7. What is his / her biggest achievements?

2nd in the Cat 3 championship in 2015 & 4th in the Cat 2 championship in 2016.

8. Was he / she difficult to train?

No

9. What's your favourite offspring of his / her?

Has many offspring , such as Raiko Van de Suikerdijk, Troy Van de Suikerdijk, U'Duvel Van de Suikerdijk, Riky Van de Suikerdijk and Thor Van de Suikerdijk, all of them known in our sport.

10. How heavy was or is he / she?

30 kg

11. Where is your training club and decoys who helped him / her?

Zwijdrecht (Belgium) decoy Sven Pultyn and DTC Ghoy, decoy Joris Christoph.

12. If you have the same dog again, what will you so different?

Nothing she has always worked well.

13. Is he / she social with people?

Yes.

14. Any funny stories you want to share?

N/A.

15. If you can change 1 thing about the dog, what would it be?

Maybe the bite

16. How was the dog like when he/ she as a puppy?

Always a happy dog and want to work.

17. How was he / she like as he / she matured?

Stable dog.

18. How are the dog's litter mates?

The same as Pep and Pio.

19. Is he / she social with other dogs?

Yes no problem.

20. Does the dog live in a house or a kennel?

Previously in kennel, now inside.

Dog 30 – Otto (BRN33067)

Owner: Jeroen Wilts and Mirella Veenstra

Full brother of my Gunther but 2 years younger. Otto is an extreme high drive dog in both biting and searching. He is social and very enthusiastic but also dominant. He's good with our other dogs, especially with puppies but dominant with strange dogs. He does everything with 200%! The combination Kuno x Bonnie, bred by Fons Vermeulen was repeated three times (now it's not possible anymore). ALL the dogs turned out to be exceptional! We owned dogs of all three breedings. Till now Otto has covered two females and the offspring looks very promising.

Add this please. Intention was to go to the fall trial this year for his PH1 but due to Corona we go next year.

Dog 31 – Rex (BRN26070)

Owner: Brent Alvey

Rex PH1 titled Malinois is a very serious, dominant, dog and a thick 90lbs.

He has a monster bite with the intent to hurt what he's biting, not just simply biting because I've seen him find a weak spot in a suit and hit the same spot every time after. Even if he's exhausted he will turn up his bite pressure and aggression if the decoy is hurting. He truly enjoys hurting decoys.

Being a larger thick type malinois has not affected his athleticism. He still springs in his legs which to me is very important and speed.

His hunt is excellent. And he is very clear headed.

The downside is he's a handful, you must be very fair when training. Many people say they want a dog like this till they meet one. You cannot have ego while handling and living with such a dog.

The thing that impresses me the most about Rex is he can perform any scenario and power through it like he's done it 100x before. I've never seen his grip change with pressure. His nerves have continued to show very strong and unwavering.

He has what I believe is true dominant aggression. Not something we see too often. Rex really does believe he is the king, which means he can be difficult to handle.

Rex is a one man type dog. He can be out in public without reaction but no one can touch him but me.

This is the type of dog I breed for but I think it's best to get them younger and deal with any unwanted behaviours right away to set yourself up for success.

1 story I always remember so far, is the day I got him. We got home around 5am after 2 days of straight driving. After a little sleep, some of my other dogs started barking, when I opened my bedroom door there was Rex in my hallway standing there. I shut the door going oh shit! I opened the door again, this time Rex growled at me. Fuck, I closed the door and reopened for a 3rd time, lucky I read up on dutch commands alittle before getting him and told him to lay down which he did. I walked past him to get some treats. He followed me to the kitchen where I tossed him a treat, it bounced off his nose, he growled at me again which was super fun! Since that didn't work I headed down to the basement where his crate was at the time. Somehow I managed to connect a leash to his flat collar. After a few failed running attempts at getting him in his crate he noticed an IPO sleeve and swallowed it by the back barrow which was even more exciting. I walked him around saying good boy Rex, good boy. I finally got him to out the sleeve and managed to get him in his crate. Not even owning him for 24hrs and we had an interesting start.

Dog 32 – Bram (BRN18061)

Owner: Ryan Geraghty

I took Bram to my place when he was a puppy. Bram was a very relaxed and confident puppy. At ten week Bram bites on the suit with a full grip. At the age of eight months Bram asked for work. I started his training. Bram was a fast learner and he loves to train. At the age of 18 months Bram knows the PH1 programme. Because I wanted Bram to be stable at all exercises I took the PH1 trial when he was three years old. Erwin Coolen, Bert Lamers, Marco Jansen and Cees van Nistelrooy are also helping me with thinking what's the best training for Bram. I have learned a lot from them.

In May 2012, I wanted to take the PH1 trial but Bram was hit by a car and had to recover six weeks. The accident took place in March. Because Bram was steady in his exercises I still went to do his PH1 trial in May. I got 437 points. Two weeks after this trial I got 440 points (full) at the selection competition for the championship. In 2012 I took 7th place in the championship. After that, Bram was going to the Dutch police.

In 2017 Bram got a new owner, Mr Ryan Geraghty, because the police can't handle Bram any more. Ryan offers me in 2018 to get Bram back for a while so he can go to the PH2 trial in the Netherlands. Bram was almost nine years old then. The moment that Bram and I see each other I never forget. It was in the early morning when I opened the door from the car. Bram saw me and yelled a lot. The dog was so happy. Bram only has one handler, the rest of his owners he tolerated.

After eight weeks training I took the PH2 trial and got 438 points.

Short description:

Stable in mind, social to people to a certain level, great courage, great grip and always want to train.

Dog 33 - Seven

Owner: Georgia Stack

1. How is he / she at home, out of work?

Seven just lays around like an old lab at home. He definitely has an off switch. I do have to put him up if we have company though. He doesn't like outsiders.

2. Describe his or her character with 5 words..

He will eat you up.

3. What is his / her best quality?

His best quality is being able to think through difficult scenarios and listen to what I am saying. In PSA there are a million things going on at once and if you don't have a dog that is in tune with you and listens to 110% you aren't going to go very far.

4. What is his / her least desirable attribute?

His least desirable attribute is that he gets so spun up before a trial that I would have to exercise him almost until he dropped to be able to step on the field without him bursting into confetti and levitating all over the place. Sometimes he would still be so excited that he barked over my commands causing him not to hear what I said.

5. Is he / she one of your favourite dogs of all time?

Seven is my favorite dog of all time. There will never be anything like him again in my eyes. Truly one of a kind.

6. What is his / her favourite activity?

Biting! There is nothing this dog would rather do than go after a bad guy. He also loves to swim and will play ball or tug until your arm falls off. Oh and car rides so he can snoot the wind.

7. What is his / her biggest achievements?

Seven's biggest achievement is becoming the world's 13th ever PSA 3 by only 3 years old. I was told he is the youngest PSA 3 in history.

8. Was he / she difficult to train?

Seven and I had a time where I felt hopeless in his training. I could not get him to calm down enough to listen to me. He would get completely out of control. At one trial in particular he went after the judge (twice). Thank god we have a flawless call off. I finally figured out a system that worked with him and the rest is history.

9. What's your favourite offspring of his / her?

My favorite offspring of Seven is Murphy owned by Jeff Allen. Murphy is a dark, gorgeous dog and PSA 1 National Champion.

10. How heavy was or is he / she?

Seven weighed about 65-70 pounds when we competed. Now he's around 75 or 80 because he's fat. Seven has never been a huge dog.

11. Where is your training club and decoys who helped him / her?

I trained for years with Khoi Pham at K9 Working Dogs of Dallas and I had a stint in Seattle where I trained French Ring with Puget Sound Dog Sports. I attribute our success to the mentorship and great decoys!

12. If you have the same dog again, what will you so different?

I don't think I would change a thing.

13. Is he / she social with people?

Seven is only social with a select few people. Everyone else can get bent.

14. Any funny stories you want to share?

One time after receiving his PSA3 we were walking into a home depot and a small child carrying a small windmill scared him.

15. If you can change 1 thing about the dog, what would it be?

I wish he would have stayed young forever

16. How was the dog like when he/ she as a puppy?

As a puppy he was very shy, never wagged his tail and was not friendly. He was pretty scared of strangers.

17. How was he / she like as he / she matured?

As an adult he is neutral to new people. He keeps his circle small just like his momma.

18. How are the dog's litter mates?

Unfortunately I did not keep up with the rest of his litter so I am not sure what they have achieved.

19. Is he / she social with other dogs?

Sev is very social with other dogs. He is definitely not the dogfighting kind. I can put him with any other dog and know that nothing will happen, at least on my dog's end.

20. Does the dog live in a house or a kennel?

Sev has earned the right to be a house dog now. He sleeps in my room every night

Dog 34 – Feloyn (UKC P655-748)

Owner: Megan Hamby

1. How is he / she at home, out of work?

Feloyn has an amazing "off-switch". Outside of work she is great to go hiking with, go to patio restaurants, or even just relax at home. She sleeps in bed and plays with our cats. She does like to steal pillow/dish towels from time to time to bring to you to tug with, though.

2. Describe his or her character with 5 words..

Driven, stable, attentive, social, and confident.

3. What is his / her best quality?

Among her many great qualities her best is how clear headed she is. She is able to adapt to the situation at hand and switch gears from bite work to obedience to being neutral.

4. What is his / her least desirable attribute?

For me, there is no trait that I would consider undesirable that she has. That being said, we have had our struggles in training because of who she is. Everything is a "game" to her; she is not a "serious" dog, so being creative with her more defensive-based scenario training was a must (unsuited muzzle work).

5. Is he / she one of your favourite dogs of all time?

She will forever be my favorite dog of all time. She is my true unicorn and I know I'll never have another her. She was my first dog I ever competed with and is always exceeding my expectations.

6. What is his / her favourite activity?

Her favorite activity, besides bite work, is being next to me with some type of a toy in her mouth.

7. What is his / her biggest achievements?

I think her most impressive achievement is her versatility in titles. At 6 years old she became the 17th dog in history to close out the PSA3 title. We then switched to French Ring and closed out her FR2 just two years later. After that, we switched to IGP and she earned her GPR3. Feloyn has been on the podium almost her entire career and earned special awards for having the highest obedience, highest protection, and being the decoys' favorite dog.

8. Was he / she difficult to train?

Overall, she is not difficult to train; she understands new behaviors quickly and is rather compliant. She is very clear headed, which makes it that much easier to work with her.

9. What's your favourite offspring of his / her?

Unfortunately, Feloyn was never able to be bred. We attempted 3 breedings, but after seeing a specialist we learned that she had pyometra and it was recommended that I spay her.

10. How heavy was or is he / she?

She is on the smaller side at 45lbs. She is quite muscular, though, underneath her slightly fluffy coat.

11. Where is your training club and decoys who helped him / her?

We are located in St. Louis, Missouri, USA and belong to Gateway Working Dog Association. Many people have helped us along the way, but Dave van Garderen, Jeremy Ciepluch, Andy Krueger, Jake Plascencia, and Jake Kemp have played huge rolls in her training and success.

12. If you have the same dog again, what will you so different?

If I had the chance to have another Feloyn, I would not change anything. I love who she is and who she has become. She has her quirks, but I wouldn't have it any other way.

13. Is he / she social with people?

Feloyn loves people! She is able and more than willing to go everywhere with me. She does demonstrations with me at schools with kids as young as elementary and enjoys all the love they shower her with.

14. Any funny stories you want to share?

She makes me laugh everyday. She is so goofy and puppy-like even at 10 years old. When she makes mistakes at training or trials, it's almost always comical. (Like bringing me the placed food on the field instead of the thrown retrieve item once at a French Ring trial) She has been known to play with her tail or try to sneakily steal your water bottle to play with too.

15. If you can change 1 thing about the dog, what would it be?

I really don't think I would change anything about her. She has what some would consider flaws but that hasn't stopped us from achieving so much. She may not be perfect in anyone else's eyes, but she is to me.

16. How was the dog like when he/ she as a puppy?

As a puppy she was a handful. She was able to overcome anything with her food and prey drive which made training as a puppy easier.

17. How was he / she like as he / she matured?

With maturity her ability to think through more stressful situations has improved. Her level of training has enabled her to think through more complex scenarios.

18. How are the dog's litter mates?

No answers

19. Is he / she social with other dogs?

She is social with other dogs to an extent. She is great with puppies and neutral with other dogs but never seeks out to play.

20. Does the dog live in a house or a kennel?

She lives in the house and is out while we are home, but crated when left. She does go to work with me every day also.

ALL CREATURES PHOTOGRAPHY

Dog 35 - Vrijheid's G Fosco (UKC P646- 104)

Owner: Steve Robert

1. How is he / she at home, out of work?

Having Fosco inside the home in the beginning was always an adventure! He has always been a high energy dog with food being his kryptonite, he could constantly get into the trash and any treats lying around! Over the last few years after his retirement he's slowed down quite a bit, now roams the house freely hoping for an intruder to bring him back to his glory days! Outside of doing work, Fosco has always been such a goofball, 90 pounds of muscle that always wants affection and is happy to hang on the couch and watch football!

2. Describe his or her character with 5 words..

Protector, alpha, beast, champion, bestfriend

3. What is his / her best quality?

Fosco has always been a dog who is willing to learn and wants to please, I pushed him harder than any dog I have ever owned. He gave me everything he had, always.

4. What is his / her least desirable attribute?

Controlling this dog around any body of water is nearly impossible!

5. Is he / she one of your favourite dogs of all time?

He is my favorite working dog of all time!

6. What is his / her favourite activity?

Fosco's favorite activities are bitework and dock diving.

7. What is his / her biggest achievements?

2014 PSA3 National Champion, at the time was the youngest dog to achieve a PSA 3.

8. Was he / she difficult to train?

Fosco was definitely stubborn at first, once we developed a strong relationship teaching new things was very simple. He's always been a very clear headed dog.

9. What's your favourite offspring of his / her?

I've only bred him once at this point, but his son Kano is heading right in his dad's paw steps.

10. How heavy was or is he / she?

Fosco is currently 82 pounds, during his PSA career he was about 90 pounds.

11. Where is your training club and decoys who helped him / her?

We started Mass Working Dogs, then ventured to Machine Shop K9. Very thankful for my decoys Josh Knowlton, Mike

Wandell, Jeff Ricco, Nick Hodgen, and my mentor John Johnston for showing me the passion of dogs.

12. If you have the same dog again, what will you so different?

I would have slowed the process down if I could have done it again, I was in such a rush to prove to the world we have what it takes. Regret that all the time, enjoy the process with your dog and treasure every time you get to step on the field.

13. Is he / she social with people?

Fosco was very suspicious to people right away, did a lot of socializing with him to get him to be a social dog. If you push him he will let you know, but if you're cool he's cool.

14. Any funny stories you want to share?

Fosco was always the dog I would use to humble people, people would come and watch bite work and say "if it came down to it, I could totally take that dog". We would put them in suits and let Fosco do his job, long story short, all changed their opinion on the situation.

15. If you can change 1 thing about the dog, what would it be?

I would make it so Fosco could never age. He's my best buddy and most loyal companion, seeing him get older breaks my heart. Would do anything to have a 5 year old Fosco forever.

16. How was the dog like when he/ she as a puppy?

Fosco was a good pup, only peed in the house once as a puppy! He was always wanting to work and play ball. Didn't care too much about bitework in the beginning, would rather attack legs and hands.

17. How was he / she like as he / she matured?

Fosco matured very quickly and became very dominant very quickly, always presented himself as the top dog and still hasn't let it go.

18. How are the dog's litter mates?

I've kept up on Facebook with a few of his litter mates. I know two became police k9s, two did search and rescue, one was donated to Penn State University.

19. Is he / she social with other dogs?

Fosco is very social with other dogs, one of his best qualities. Would constantly use him at my business K-9 Top Performance to help reactive dogs, as well as in home visits.

20. Does the dog live in a house or a kennel?

Happy to say that Fosco is now retired and enjoying the freedom of the house and whatever couch he would like to lounge in. I think he's earned it!

Dog 36 – Luko (BRN26199)

Owner: Sandra Arguello Younker

Luko is my pet first and my protector 2nd. At home he is a big baby, in fact many jokingly call him Baby Wuko. Luko goes almost everywhere with me. He goes shopping, to concerts, flies all over the USA with me for work, and even goes to the local bars with me. He is all around a loving dog. Is probably the most social with people and animals.

Luko in 5 words: clear-headed, protector, social, aware, dependable.

Luko's best quality to me is how he looks at me. I have never had a dog look at me like his life depends on it.

His least desirable attribute is that he won't live as long as me. Aside from that he is a talker, he likes to sassy me and argue with me on and off the field.

Luko is the beat of my heart, the air that I breathe, the spirit of my soul. There is not a dog out there now or in the future that will ever be able to fill his shoes to me.

He loves when we do searches. Whether it is with me playing hide-n-seek or searching for a decoy. The moment he knows he is going to do a search he gets this concentration in his eyes that ignites me.

I am hoping getting our level 3 will be our biggest achievement, but for now our biggest achievement is not having a single fail between our PDC and level 2.

Our biggest training challenge would have been the change position. For some reason something clicked in his head and he just could not hold the position.

My favorite offspring, he has only had 1 litter but I would say it was Kodiak owned by Megan Fowler. He is a spitting image of Luko and has many characteristics of his.

Luko in the winter weighs about 80-85 and in the summer it is 75-80.

I am with K9 Working Dogs of Dallas. My primary decoys are Khoi Pham, Tim Akers, and Josh Kirby; but we also have Colten Erbe, Kim Balega, Chad Vivanco and David Parrish.

If I cloned Luko I am not sure I would do anything different. He was the very first dog I have ever trained. I just think I have more experience now and would be a better trainer for him.

Luko as a puppy was amazing. My club often says I lucked out. He never chewed, he slept in his crate quietly while potty training him, he was always attentive, was super calm, and learned fairly quickly. I could easily take him on the field and he would patiently wait his turn to train; the moment it was his turn he would light up and be a working dog and then easily return to my pet. I for the most part have never really crated him, just haven't had to. Luko all around has been very consistent; puppy Luko and adult Luko are very much the same.

Funny story:

I had a storage unit in my backyard that had a mouse in it and I was trying to kill it. I had brought Luko out in hopes if the mouse ran the opposite direction as me Luko would kill it. As I was moving everything the mouse ran straight to Luko, my protector.. My vicious dog.. My Luko saw that mouse running at him and he jumped straight in the air and when he landed he ran behind me. Needless to say the mouse got away and couldn't stop laughing at Luko.

Proudest Characters of Luko: One of the things Luko is the most known for and I am the proudest for is his call-off. Luko has a 15-foot launch. Some scenarios the call off cone is 10-12 feet; which means Luko has already launched for his bite. Luko is known for having his mouth completely targeted and committed on a decoys bicep for a bite, he can be inches from biting and hear me call him off and has closed his mouth and body checked the decoy with no bite. It's one of the most amazing things to witness.

Dog 37 - Aramis Red Fevils Dog (SPKP4084)

Owner: Pavol šlahor

1. How is he / she at home, out of work?

At home he is calm, child friendly.

2. Describe his or her character with 5 words..

He has dominant character, confident property, predatory.

3. What is his / her best quality?

Defense with strong innate bite and militancy.

4. What is his / her least desirable attribute?

He doesn't want to share with anybody.

5. Is he / she one of your favourite dogs of all time?

The second best.

6. What is his / her favourite activity?

His favourite discipline is defense and swimming.

7. What is his / her biggest achievements?

His success: MSFCI- 4th place in world cup FMBB, 6th place FMBB 2018, best defence in FMBB 2018, when he was 2.5 years old he was Slovak champion.

8. Was he / she difficult to train?

He learned quickly, when he was 2.5 years old he had IPO3.

9. What's your favourite offspring of his / her?

BEST defence in FMBB 2018.

10. How heavy was or is he / she?

36kg.

11. Where is your training club and decoys who helped him / her?

It's not a club, we are good friends.

12. If you have the same dog again, what will you so different?

Another method of submission training.

13. Is he / she social with people?

Yes.

14. Any funny stories you want to share?

Funny with the passage of time, in defence in world championship he decided not to come off a bite and I had to use 5 more commands, so because of this we lost relevant points.

15. If you can change 1 thing about the dog, what would it be?

Less dominance.

16. How was the dog like when he/ she as a puppy?

Active, talented, learned quickly.

17. How was he / she like as he / she matured?

Social, dominant, teachable.

18. How are the dog's litter mates?

His brother.

19. Is he / she social with other dogs?

Yes.

20. Does the dog live in a house or a kennel?

In the kennel.

Dog 38 - Lorockmor Paco (BRN24116)

Owner: Ian Morgan

1. How is he / she at home, out of work?

Paco is a lovely affectionate dog with me, if we go for a walk and I stand still he will always come and jump up on me and nuzzle into me for some fuss and attention.

2. Describe his or her character with 5 words..

Dominant, confident, alpha, leader, powerful.

3. What is his / her best quality?

Paco has so many qualities but one of his best is his heart and determination, his willingness to keep going forward no matter the pressure or environment he is in, he just has a tunnel vision for the target that's in front of him.

4. What is his / her least desirable attribute?

Paco's least desirable trait has to be the fact you can not leave anything in the kennel with him as he will destroy everything.

5. Is he / she one of your favourite dogs of all time?

Paco is 100% my favourite dog that I have ever owned or seen for that matter. I know I'm going to be biased but honestly he is special.

6. What is his / her favourite activity?

Paco's favourite activity is definitely bite work. He would rather bite than mate a female all day long he lives for bite work.

7. What is his / her biggest achievements?

Paco's biggest achievement had to be achieving his PH1 with a score of 425 followed closely by winning Avd gold class in the uk in 2018 with the biggest number of entries ever there being 16 dogs in a very high pressure gold class and he was the stand out winner.

8. Was he / she difficult to train?

Danny Giesen from the Netherlands trained him for his PH1 title and from the stories he's told me Paco was not an easy dog to train, trying to control the drive was very difficult but once I brought him and started training things for the UK trial scene things were relatively straightforward as he has such great desire for the bite work and less control being needed.

9. What's your favourite offspring of his / her?

My favourite offspring would have to be Mensa, big strong powerful male with great drives and work ethic , I also like another son of his called Dino from the Celiks Home Larna breeding.

10. How heavy was or is he / she?

Paco weighed 36kg fit.

11. Where is your training club and decoys who helped him / her?

My training club is Lorockmor Working Dogs and the main decoy to help me with Paco's training at the time was Paul Harding, I also had help from the following decoys Laurie Stanley, Asa Wright, Dalton Rush and Will Holmes.

12. If you have the same dog again, what will you so different?

If I had Paco again there's not much I'd do differently as he's worked out perfectly for me.

13. Is he / she social with people?

I would not class Paco as social with people or civil he is impartial but I know for sure he will not tolerate any corrections or rough handling from anyone .

14. Any funny stories you want to share?

I don't really have any comical stories about Paco as he's not that type of character, he's quite straight laced and serious.

15. If you can change 1 thing about the dog, what would it be?

The only thing I can think of I'd change is it would be nice if he was a little bit bigger.

16. How was the dog like when he/ she as a puppy?

From what I'm told Paco was crazy as a puppy , he was biting an adult IPO sleeve at the age of 6 weeks old.

17. How was he / she like as he / she matured?

As a mature dog Paco oozes confidence, struts around like he owns the place wherever he goes with his trademark scorpion tail sticking up, scanning the horizon for potential troublemakers.

18. How are the dog's litter mates?

There's two of his litter mates in particular that stand out one being Butch a titled male that has competed at the national championships twice and a sister called Bonnie that has been a great producer of working dogs.

19. Is he / she social with other dogs?

Paco is not social with other males at all but is social with females but is definitely the boss, for example if he is taking a drink and a female comes to take a drink out of the same bowl, he will see them off with great ferocity.

20. Does the dog live in a house or a kennel?

Paco currently lives outside in the kennel block.

Dog 39 - Lorockmor Mensa (BRN32831)

Owner: Ian Morgan

1. How is he / she at home, out of work?

Mensa is a very pleasant and easy dog out of work, quiet and clean in the kennel and generally pretty relaxed.

2. Describe his or her character with 5 words..

Strong, confident, neutral, social and happy.

3. What is his / her best quality?

Mensa's best quality is his willingness to work and the way he can handle pressure.

4. What is his / her least desirable attribute?

Least desirable attribute is a difficult one, maybe the fact he can be aggressive with other mature males.

5. Is he / she one of your favourite dogs of all time?

Mensa is definitely one of my favourites, I bred him myself so have seen the journey from day one and he just keeps ticking the boxes for me.

6. What is his / her favourite activity?

Mensa loves to swim, when I take him to a local pool to do some swimming, he just dives in without needing to be told and he'll just keep swimming around and having a great time.

7. What is his / her biggest achievements?

Achievements with Mensa is an awkward one. As a very young dog he was doing things that older more experienced dogs were struggling with, he took everything in his stride from a very young age. The biggest achievement will really be if I can get my PH1 title with him as I did lots of crazy work with him up until he was approximately 22 months old when I came to the decision that he was too good a dog to just keep doing UK type trials. He had too much talent to waste on that type of work so that's when I made the decision to try to train him in the KNPV program. At first it was an extremely hard transition to make due to the level of control that is needed but we are now making steady progress.

8. Was he / she difficult to train?

Difficult to train, yes and no. Not difficult in the sense that he has so much natural genetic talent but on the other hand yes it's been difficult to train him because of the things I did with him in the early stages with him and then had to change everything to pursue KNPV with him.

9. What's your favourite offspring of his / her?

Mensa is still young so not many offspring old enough for me to judge him on but I do have a nice son of his from the pixel breeding which I'm hoping will be my next KNPV dog.

10. How heavy was or is he / she?

38kg fit.

11. Where is your training club and decoys who helped him / her?

My training club is Lorockmor Working Dogs, in the early days the decoys that helped me progress with Mensa were Paul Harding and Asa Wright. The last 18 months since switching to KNPV it has been Sam Frost, Laurie Stanley, Erwin Coolen, Andy Boyen and Jack Delissen.

12. If you have the same dog again, what will you so different?

There's not much I'd do differently if I had him from a pup again.

13. Is he / she social with people?

As a younger dog he wasn't social with people but since switching to KNPV it's something I've had to work very hard to do, seeing as I need help from a second man in the training program.

14. Any funny stories you want to share?

The story that sticks out in my mind is my first trip to Holland with him on my very first KNPV training trip with him. We met up with Danny Giesen and went to train the dogs in the swimming exercise across a canal, Andrea went first with Hanzo, all went well then it was my turn with Mensa. I got to the water edge and told him to go over, he dived in like a pro and started to power across the water. There were a few comments about how powerfully he was swimming, he then got to the bank the other side, climbed out, ran and bit Danny full on the leg! We were all in shock, Danny was screaming and it was chaos! We got him off and back across the water, Danny was absolutely fuming but luckily not too badly injured.

15. If you can change 1 thing about the dog, what would it be?

If I could change one thing about him it would be that he took off better for his long sends, it's always nice to see a dog that flies.

16. How was the dog like when he/ she as a puppy?

Mensa as a puppy, well it was fate that I ended up with him. I'd taken reservations for the litter and originally I'd planned to keep a male but then as the pups got to around 4/5 weeks there was a female that was really catching my eye so I made the decision that she'd be my keeper. The pups were now 8 weeks and ready for there new homes so I contacted the people who'd made the reservations in order of pick that they had got, I then came to the last pick so I rang Gary and said something along the lines of " Hi Gary, your pup is ready, he's a nice pup I think you'll like him" to which Gary's reply was " He? I reserved a female" as soon as he said it my heart sank and I realized my mistake and quickly scanned back through my phone to check my messages and there it was he'd ordered a female. Me being a man of my word I said to Gary "Well today is your lucky day because you've gone from last pick female to pick of the litter female" which he was obviously very happy with and I ended up with last pick male which was Mensa! But he was a great puppy and excelled at everything I asked of him

17. How was he / she like as he / she matured?

Mensa has matured into a super impressive dog in my opinion not only in looks and structure but also in his work and currently only two and a half years old I think there's more to come.

18. How are the dog's litter mates?

His breeding (Paco x Chloe) has been repeated 4 times and that's how impressive this combination has been. There are several offsprings in police and prison roles, some in training for KNPV and some in the USA and Holland. I also own a litter brother and a sister from the following litter.

19. Is he / she social with other dogs?

Mensa is social with other dogs but not other mature males.

20. Does the dog live in a house or a kennel?

Mensa lives outside in the kennel block.

Dog 40 - Stateline's Danny Zuko (AKC DN24843401)

Owner: **Janet dooley Edwards**

1. How is he / she at home, out of work?

Danny is naturally a great house dog and very clear headed outside of work. Very social and has been used many times for school demos with kids.

2. Describe his or her character with 5 words..

I always say that Danny's motto in life is "Go hard or go home". He does everything at extreme. Extreme in his work, extreme in his sociability and extreme in his tolerance.

3. What is his / her best quality?

His best quality is his stability and clear headedness. On the field, his powerful entries are what he is best known for. All decoys were a mix of excited and intimidated to catch Danny on a trial field.

4. What is his / her least desirable attribute?

His least desirable quality is that he is an escape artist- he will break out of almost anything, jump fences, open doors to get out when he wants. Again following the motto "go hard or go home"

5. Is he / she one of your favourite dogs of all time?

He is definitely a favorite. I really got lucky having a dog that is strong enough to blow through PSA 3 Protection routines and yet be so social outside of work.

6. What is his / her favourite activity?

Bite work is by far his favorite activity.

7. What is his / her biggest achievements?

PSA 3- I believe he is the only dog to have passed his first leg on only his second attempt and earned both legs of the title in one trial season.

8. Was he / she difficult to train?

His control with the strong decoy presence in PSA was tough but outside of that he loved obedience and learning new things.

9. What's your favourite offspring of his / her?

I'm still waiting for most of his offspring to mature but so far he has thrown good working dogs with good temperaments, carrying his nice balance, with all females. They have been successful in everything from PSA, French Ring, detection, SAR, and internationally ranked in frisbee.

10. How heavy was or is he / she?

His prime working weight was about 72 lbs.

11. Where is your training club and decoys who helped him / her?

All of Danny's training was at our Stateline Canine PSA Club with my husband doing all of his foundation bite work.

12. If you have the same dog again, what will you so different?

I don't know that I would change anything that I did with another dog like Danny.

13. Is he / she social with people?

If I could change one thing about Danny, it would be that he contained much better in a crate, kennel, etc.

14. Any funny stories you want to share?

Danny showed to be a strong/solid puppy and was sold at 12 weeks old. The original buyer planned to train him in protection but never did because he did not have time to commit to it. I was asked if I was interested in taking him back when he was 2 years old since he was not able to train/ work him. That's another thing that is impressive about Danny; he was just a house dog and at 2 years started training for PSA like he never missed a day of training in his life.

15. If you can change 1 thing about the dog, what would it be?

Danny has 3 littermates that are titled in PSA, 1 of them also has a PSA 3 title.

16. How was the dog like when he/ she as a puppy?

In Danny's first 2 years as a house dog, he had playdates with other dogs and has excellent social skills. However, he is very dominant and will make sure he is at the top of the pecking order.

Dog 41 - Cartuck van Joefarm (LOSH948824)

Owner: Janet Dooley Edwards

1. How is he / she at home, out of work?

Zuko took a while to settle in the house. Until he was about 5 his house time was pretty restricted to a place bed. Once he was past 5, he was extremely calm and good in the house.

2. Describe his or her character with 5 words..

Zuko was an independent, high prey drive dog.

3. What is his / her best quality?

I would say that Zuko's best quality was his nerves. Nothing phased him so my errors as a brand new handler and anything new in training never set him back.

4. What is his / her least desirable attribute?

His worst quality to me was that he didn't love obedience. It took A LOT of repetition for anything in obedience to stick with him.

5. Is he / she one of your favourite dogs of all time?

Zuko was my heart dog. He did anything and everything that I asked of him and we developed an amazing bond.

6. What is his / her favourite activity?

With no doubt this dog loved to bite more than anything.

7. What is his / her biggest achievements?

His obedience was not easy to train but became better and better as our bond grew. He was not soft but responsive to corrections so control was stable with him. He learned very quickly when it came to bite work.

8. Was he / she difficult to train?

Zuko has an impressive resumé. He earned his PSA 3 title, only the 9th dog to earn that accomplishment. He is a 3x National Champion in PSA. The sport created an award after his accomplishment of winning Nationals at ALL levels in the sport called the Mount Everest Award, and currently he is the ONLY dog to have earned that. He was inducted into the PSA Hall of Fame in 2016. He won many other awards in the sport throughout his career to include High in Trial, High Obedience, High Protection, High Overall for the trial year. He was also certified in narcotics detection through the NTPDA working privately and assisting law enforcement.

9. What's your favourite offspring of his / her?

Zuko likely has the most titled offspring in PSA. So far, 2 of them have a PSA 3 title and 1 more is currently competing in the 3s and even more are still training to be there. No other sire has had that many offspring in the highest level of the sport. His offspring have won many High Protection, High in Trial, Top Dog and Highest Overall Scores in a season. He has offspring as Police K9s and is titled in French Ring as well. So many of them are impressive that it's tough to pick one favorite.

10. How heavy was or is he / she?

Zuko's competition weight was 65 lbs.

11. Where is your training club and decoys who helped him / her?

Most of Zuko's training was at Tarheel Canine Training in Sanford, NC. I moved to Pennsylvania at the end of his career where my husband, Shawn Edwards, was his decoy.

12. If you have the same dog again, what will you so different?

I don't like to look back and change the way that I did anything. I was a brand new handler for a competition dog and I know that I made a lot of mistakes and had to learn a lot as I went. But that is how this process works. We always have a lot to learn as trainers and handlers and that is why I enjoy this journey.

13. Is he / she social with people?

Zuko was very social. He was never exposed to children young so he did see small kids as prey when they were acting in a manner to trigger the prey drive. Once I had a child and he had the exposure, that went away.

14. Any funny stories you want to share?

I also joked that Zuko had a 'limp reflex". He just loved any affection so if you touched him, he went limp and would lean or lay on you. Even at the vet's office for x-rays or examining injuries. You could literally do anything to that dog and he would just stay limp as long as you were touching him.

15. If you can change 1 thing about the dog, what would it be?

I wouldn't change anything about Zuko. I'm biased at this point as we had accomplished so much together and grew an incredible bond and working relationship, so I really grew to love everything about him.

16. How was the dog like when he/ she as a puppy?

Zuko was a wild puppy. Bit anything and everything and was never sensitive to being corrected or pulled off of anything. That's when I knew he was the perfect dog for PSA.

17. How was he / she like as he / she matured?

Maturity did Zuko very well. The more he matured, the more he settled on the trial field and in the house.

18. How are the dog's litter mates?

I don't know any of his littermates but his father is a well known stud dog for Euro Joe, Urosh van Joefarm. And he is the grandson of Elgos du Chemin des Plaines. I was extremely lucky to have a dog so tightly bred to Elgos as he was such a well known producer. And the genetics have shown to produce strong dogs in Zuko's offspring as well.

19. Is he / she social with other dogs?

Zuko was dog social to the dog's he knew. Otherwise he was more neutral to dogs.

20. Does the dog live in a house or a kennel?

He lived in the house once he was ⅚.

Dog 42 – Flits (BRN30789)

Owner: Alan mcAdam

1) How is he at home out of work?

When Flits is at home out of work he is a very protective dog of his home. He craves attention and affection from his family, he can be very destructive so he needs to be kept in his pen when not supervised.

2) Describe his character in 5 words?

Intelligent, Mischievous, Robust, Protective and Lovable.

3) What is his best quality?

Flits' best quality would be his eagerness to please as he does everything with all his heart.

4) What is his least desirable attribute?

Flits' least desirable attribute would be his destructiveness, he will destroy anything you leave with him.

5) Is he one of your favourite dogs of all times?

Yes, Flits would be one of my favourite dogs of all times as I have bred him and trained him from a pup to achieve his PH1 certification at 2.5 years old.

6) What is his favourite activity?

Flits loves to swim, he also loves to do bite work.

7) What is his biggest achievement?

Flits' biggest achievement was being trained in Ireland from a pup and completing his Ph1 training. He then went to Holland on the 5th October 2019 and achieved his PH1 certificate at 2.5 years old. On this day he has made history in Ireland becoming the 1st dog bred and trained in Ireland to obtain a PH1 certification.

8) Was he difficult to train?

Flits has had his moments in training like any high drive dog. He was very possessive over the decoy in the transport exercise and in the reveir of the decoy as he tried to intimidate the decoy to move. He does everything with so much heart and drive it can be difficult at times.

9) What's your favourite offspring of his?

Flits has no offspring yet!

10) How heavy was/is he?

Flits weighs 40.7 kg now. He was 38 kg at his PH1 trial.

11) Where is your training club and decoys who helped him?

We train in Newcastle, County Dublin, Ireland. Up to 16 months old I did all the decoy work with Flits, my wife and children handled him. Later on in his training Michael Kelly did some of the decoy work.

12) If you have the same dog again what will you do differently?

If I had the same dog again I would do more training sessions and train with more distractions around the dog. I would also attend more pre-trials in Holland.

13) Is he social with people?

Flits is social on the training field as he knows this is work and we work as a team, when training is finished he is not social anymore.

14) Any funny stories you want to share?

No, none I can think of.

15) If you can change 1 thing about the dog what would it be?

There is nothing I would change about Flits. He is an amazing all round dog that will do anything that is asked of him.

16) How was the dog like when he was a puppy?

Flits as a puppy was full of character and mischief. He was very enthusiastic. He was very possessive of anything that he could get his teeth into. He always won over my family with his charismatic behaviour and those puppy dog eyes.

17) How was he like when he matured?

Flits is now just over 3 years old, he still hasn't matured fully. He is as driven as a young dog full of enthusiasm. He doesn't slow down and maybe he never will.

18) How are the dogs litter mates?

Some of Flits litter mates are in the UK, as far as I'm aware a lot of them are excelling in their type of training and work.

19) Is he social with other dogs?

Yes. Flits is very social with other dogs, males and females. He is extremely gentle with puppies and young dogs which gives them a nice experience with an older dog.

20) Does he live in a house or kennel?

Flits lives in his kennel as he is destructive, he does not relax in the house as all he wants to do is work. So for this reason he lives in his kennel. He comes into the house during the day to keep him connected with the family.

5 / October / 2019

Flits BRN 30789

Flits BRN 30789

Dog 43 - Arco Verbeek (BRN30789)

Owner: marcell Patterson

1. How is he / she at home, out of work?

At home Arco is very easily managed. When I'm away my daughter handles him with no problem. When people see him they say it's hard to believe he is a police dog.

2. Describe his or her character with 5 words..

Character: Strong, Intense, unbreakable, and social.

3. What is his / her best quality?

Arco's best quality is that as strong as he is in the work, when work is over he is super social. He switches from work to play and back to work easily. It's very hard to describe this dog. Words don't do him justice.

4. What is his / her least desirable attribute?

His least desirable attribute would have to be his ability to endure and withstand harsh corrections. He is impossible to break in the work.

5. Is he / she one of your favourite dogs of all time?

Arco is easily my favorite dog of all time. I don't get emotionally attached to dogs but Arco is the exception. Every person gets a once in a lifetime dog and Arco is mine.

There will never be another Arco. The closest I can get to him will be one of his offspring.

6. What is his / her favourite activity?

His favorite activity would have to be eating. I've never seen a dog with food drive like his!

7. What is his / her biggest achievements?

His biggest achievement would have to be being placed in the Department of Defense breeding program. Seeing his offspring excel in the military is a special accomplishment. He has also produced several working police dogs and has numerous apprehensions of his own as a police dog. The only reason that Arco didn't obtain a PH1 certificate was because of a leg fracture that he suffered prior to the inspection.

8. Was he / she difficult to train?

Arco's initial training was done in the Netherlands by Henk Verbeek at his KNPV club PHV "De Eendracht" in Lunteren. Arco was a handful to train and when someone who has the experience of Henk Verbeek says that you know he was difficult. From my experience training with Arco for police he was difficult because he is non stop and corrections don't phase the dog. Arco is a dog that you must gain cooperation with. If you fight with him to get him to do something you will lose.

9. What's your favourite offspring of his / her?

My favorite offspring at the moment would be "Djill". She is a female that is with my police department. I saw a video of this dog in the Netherlands and thought she was super. At the time I had no idea she was an Arco offspring. Once I agreed to purchase her and received the BRN number I learned she was an Arco daughter. She has super nerves, drives, and hunt.

10. How heavy was or is he / she?

Arco is a 80 pound powerhouse of a dog.

11. Where is your training club and decoys who helped him / her?

Arco is my patrol dog with the Oakland Police Department. We train in and around the Oakland, California area and use a host of different decoys for his training. From time to time we use outside decoys such as Charlie Randolph who provides Police Training Seminars for the Police Department.

12. If you have the same dog again, what will you so different?

If I had the same dog again, there's really not much I would do differently.

13. Is he / she social with people?

Arco is extremely social. I have never seen a dog with his on/off switch. It's one of the things that make him special.

14. Any funny stories you want to share?

Funny stories: When I first got Arco I decided to take him to a local training club where the egos were big. Some decoys in the group said that most of the time when they hear about a dogs reputation the dog falls short when they work the dog. So they told me they weren't expecting much. The first three decoys were knocked to the ground and after they said "He is as advertised".

15. If you can change 1 thing about the dog, what would it be?

If I could change one thing about Arco it would be his ability to receive corrections and submit easier to corrections.

16. How was the dog like when he/ she as a puppy?

As a puppy Arco was a handful and that is how he eventually found his way to Henk Verbeek.

17. How was he / she like as he / she matured?

Arco was extremely driven with a nonstop attitude by the time he was a year old. People who saw him knew he was going to be something special.

18. How are the dog's litter mates?

Unknown about his littermates.

19. Is he / she social with other dogs?

Arco is social with all females and most males.

20. Does the dog live in a house or a kennel?

Arco is the only dog that I have ever allowed to live inside my home.

Dog 44 – Rage (BRN26658)

Owner: Rodney Stoute

From 6 weeks weighing in at 2.5kg to his current age of 5 years old, weighing in at 45kg. BVA Hip and elbow scored at 3 years old after intense work. Scoring at and even 7/7 on the hips and 0/0 on the elbows.

Rage was bred by Mr A Doeze, chosen and owned by me Mr Rodney Stoute, at RS Real Deal, Boot Camp.

Rage's litter siblings were all very good and the choice wasn't easy. His litter mates are in Holland doing well in knpv.

However, I chose Rage on both his character, and conformity, he stood out. Being black brindle with his unusual shaped head, natural intent to bite and a natural full hard grip.

After owning Rage for just a short time I was able to have him holding on to tree branches for lengths of time from his tiny strong young mouth. His confidence and focus on work ethic was second to none. Rage from a tiny little body was showing signs of being a great dog. Doing all you could with an adult but in a young puppy form.

With all these natural qualities he was also a pleasure around the home. He's easy going and a great one man dog that could live in my family home with no issues.

He is totally focused on me so children, cats, dogs people etc were of no interest to him. Although due to my own ailments Rage was mainly housed in a comfortable kennel and was accepting of this.

Rage grew into an intent and powerful male which is highly prey driven and extremely intelligent. His qualities I feel is that he's an all round level dog but with that intent or purpose.

He is a medium sized, big boned male with an unusual head shape that is very broad and powerful. He is hugely confident which makes him very versatile in character. He sees nothing as a threat unless it becomes one. He is very quick in responding and will go in strong and forward if necessary.

With the ability to read a situation well, this is what made him an excellent dog in my family home. His unique presence and the added protection if needed.

Rage as mentioned earlier was imprinted as a young pup by myself, and trained throughout the years. He won and competed in many competitions.

To name just a few:

Avd and night trials, being one of the biggest and hardest working events for your dog in the UK.

First place in, AVD long send

First place in reality service dog.

This exercise was Rage being one of several dogs put into a room alone and him being one of the few dogs reacting as he should and going straight in for a bite on the threat.

First place in silver class, night trials.

and many many more.

There are videos of him doing various real life scenarios, and sport events, on YouTube and MuMuzTV for those who want to view him.

Also just to mention the other side to rage.

Pushing prams, pushing puppies on swings, shopping, getting me a beer from the fridge, driving lawn mowers...

And I must mention in the wheelie bin and this bin was on the back of an ash cart. "The poor bin men". I thought to myself what a great opportunity to do some environmental training and stopped them in mid work. And asked them if I could do this exercise. So there they were watching me ask Rage to hop in a bin. Then voice off whilst the driver lifts the bin up with Rage inside on back of the ash wagon.

Must be seen in the video, as funny as that looked. It shows his total trust in me and his own courage. To mention courage, he also had a bite of a decoy in the back of a helicopter, no hesitation.

I could go on and on with his credibility.

But I think you get the picture of this wonderful dog. A real film star Rage could be, although he's a real protection dog also.

Rage has his world wide acknowledgement and achievements in sport. He was originally and mainly trained as my very own protection dog and that is where rage truly excelled.

Open Rage for real in a real situation and you'd see his real courage and strength. Many occasions Rage had my back in sticky situations, with no hesitation. But this boy would play the game and make me proud in sport also.

In the training of Rage he was put onto mainly "novice decoys" throughout his life which ensured Rage was not decoy dependent.

Never, was he ever equipment focused. He was a true to type protection dog.

He was taught to go for the offending body part so he would switch bite. But clean, strong impact and clamping bites on the switch. He has done environmentals to the extreme with no hesitation, putting all trust in me as the handler.

Focus is solid, obedience fast direct and fun.

Drug detection and search and retrieve.

Rage is known worldwide, he has sired quite a few litters being put to only selected females, passing great genetics on to his progenies and his level confident character, his drive, power and intent. His offsprings are very versatile also. There are many in the police force, personal, protection, sport and agility. Protecting rhinos in Africa and a small few as active pets.

I couldn't say I have a favourite offspring of his. They are all good in their own game. However I saw a specific bitch very similar to Rage but with a smaller frame that I wanted to put Rage over and see the offspring. First thought, they produced a litter of very good dogs. We kept back a bitch, Crayell Trigger, she is showing all the same credentials as the parents. One to look out for in the future. A bitch I can go back into for genetics, and keep this versatile genetics alive.

I was once asked what I would change in Rage if I could? Nothing I replied. If I had to then maybe 2 inches taller as Rage stood 25 inches to the shoulder.

But what a fabulous journey we are having. A real honest dog.

Dog 45 – Buddy (BRN34703)

Owner: Hein Van Galen

1. How is he / she at home, out of work?

Relaxed at home but always sharp and alert.

2. Describe his or her character with 5 words..

Desire to work, tough dog, relaxed out of drive, happy dog , great guarding skills.

3. What is his / her best quality?

Unstoppable drive to work.

4. What is his / her least desirable attribute?

Does not have a least desirable trait.

5. Is he / she one of your favourite dogs of all time?

Yes he is a top dog.

6. What is his / her favourite activity?

Biting.

7. What is his / her biggest achievements?

Ready for PH1.

8. Was he / she difficult to train?

Got Buddy when he was 1.5 years old, he was too much for the first handler and I took him in to train in the KNPV program.

9. What's your favourite offspring of his / her?

Pinto son of Buddy working in the USA police force.

10. How heavy was or is he / she?

43kg.

11. Where is your training club and decoys who helped him / her?

Training at the police dog club in Doetinchem Holland.

12. If you have the same dog again, what will you so different?

Nothing.

13. Is he / she social with people?

No.

14. Any funny stories you want to share?

When he is tired after work he likes to roll around in the kennel.

15. If you can change 1 thing about the dog, what would it be?

Drifts are too extreme sometimes.

16. How was the dog like when he/ she as a puppy?

What I heard from the previous handler, he was a very happy and free puppy.

17. How was he / she like as he / she matured?

Got him at 18 months old so I can not say anything about that.

18. How are the dog's litter mates?

Most litter mates are working dogs with the police.

19. Is he / she social with other dogs?

No.

20. Does the dog live in a house or a kennel?

In the kennel.

Dog 46 – Wibo (BRN10713)

Owner: Dick and Selena Van Leeuwen

Wibo is bred by Jan Mokkink out of Aron and a Rocky daughter named Nike.

We got him as a young dog with basic KNPV training. Reason he was sold is that he was way too much dog for his handler.

Wibo's character can best be described as extremely dominant, very high pain tolerance combined with easy to provoke by dominance triggers.

Natural calm pushing grip. Calm, stable character, no hecticness but the right amount of drive which should be controlled.

One man dog.

Wibo was about 40 kilo and 67 cm shoulder height.

He was bred to 32 times and mostly by us in line breeding with Rocky linebred females.

So even not bred to so very much, his rate of good offspring is good. An aspect in that is also the choices made in the females.

We handled him being a "stud" as breeders and not as stud owners so we were very selective in combinations made with him.

Also a very high percentage of his offspring are medical checked (X-rayed), because of their work as psd for example and all OK.

Wibo was no dog for an inexperienced handler.

Pushing the wrong buttons could make him untrainable and create a fight (with no winner, because surrender was no option for him).

I trained Wibo with my good friends Remco Witkamp, Kevin de Man and Edwin Sollart. Remco and Edwin were national decoys for KNPV.

Wibo was socially neutral. Even a little provocation in his dominance would light him up (eye contact for example).

Wibo had to be trained with a good feeling for dosing and timing. Pushing the wrong buttons could light him up. Keeping him low drive was essential to train him.

Wibo made the certificate for PSD. Although also trained for KNPV, no sportdog to certify within KNPV settings.

My Bassie, Pebbles are good offsprings, but Bor, Greagus, Puskas, Rocko and many more also.

Wibo was or is an important component in our breeding program that still is based on his grandfather, my Rocky (brn 1676).

261

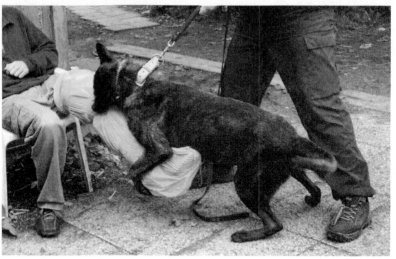

Dog 47 – Hannibal

Owner: Andre Meding

1) Hannibal is living a "pet life". There is no real difference between work or out of work, because Hannibal is not worked in common dog sports nor is he used in a job. When I do dog training I just do it as some kind of workout for the dogs. Therefore I own four dogs and he is one of the older ones, Hannibal is not trained very often lately. Hannibal is a very demanding dog within everyday life who has to be handled with a lot of consideration and foresight in public.

2) Loyal, protective, serious, sensible and different.

3) It's hard to speak about Hannibal's best qualities, because all his so-called qualities come also with disadvantages or besides with restrictions for me as the handler. Hannibal is a demanding dog not easy to handle. I could have easily written down a credible public adulation of my own dog, but I am not the kind of guy praising my own dogs and Hannibal is the kind of dog he would be, even within the working dog world, just a burden for most of the people.

In simplest terms many people would see a good protection dog in Hannibal, maybe a good police dog, also a dog who can perform on the dog field within demanding competitions. To a certain degree I would also agree, but a dog with that low threshold to being offended by people would be also too stressed within working in those areas. Also within sports such a dog can never feel that comfortable when working with the decoy. So Hannibal's best quality is just being my dog.

4) Hannibal does not like to travel. He is very nervous while travelling and even the weekly journey to the dog field half an hour away is very stressful to him. When not being in his familiar surroundings the dog does not like to eat or sleep. When being at a dog field it became a bit better, but all other journeys are very stressful for the dog.

5) Hannibal is my first dog therefore he is for sure a bit more special to me then my other three dogs.

Compared to dogs of other dog handlers I have seen many dogs performing better than Hannibal and also a lot of dogs performing not so good. All dogs have got their pros and cons, but I personally like dogs with a character like Hannibal (what for sure has got something to do that he is my first dog).

6) Like many other dogs Hannibal likes to play with balls and different toys. He is not very demanding when it comes to activities as long as he can be near me. When I had to name an activity he likes the most then it would be hanging around on the sofa and watching me playing video games while playing with his Kong.

7) Hannibal is not worked in common dog sports therefore his achievements are restricted to open freestyle events, mostly of the club AVD e.V.,

a German breeding club for working presa canarios, events for security service dogs or simple fun events. Some of them have become more and more recognized and meaningful within a growing group of working dog people who do not like the work in scheme.

Here Hannibal has won many trophies up to the highest level, f.e. he won the gold class of 5K-9 Working Dogs AVD e.V. UK event in 2015 followed by many others. Within a time frame of one year Hannibal was entered in four gold classes of the AVD e.V. (two of them in the UK) where he came off three times on the podium.

His biggest achievement is the fact that compared to many other dogs Hannibal was always able to perform on the same level again after a build up.

Within constancy I have seen a lot of better dogs performing on the dog field then Hannibal, f.e. Satvinder Gills Bang Bang von der Lönshütte or Ian Morgans Paco, but on a good day Hannibal does not have to hide.

Another of his achievements is the fact that Hannibal's performances in 2015 from my point of view for sure are one of the reasons for a little hype of malinois/herders within the UKs dog event scene.

8) As we don't do common dog sports my answers are limited to the things we train. Hannibal's attention is very short as he has got no huge will to please. When I do "train" some obedience for fun I have to do all exercises on leash out of security reasons. Besides Hannibal is a very quick learning dog.

9) Hannibal was a stud male to two females of three litters in overall. The malinois Bente von der Lönshütte was mated to him twice and the x-herder Chilly von der Bielefelder Burg once. Out of these combinations there are promising dogs handled within IGP, security service, as rescue dog, but also just active companion dogs.

From the dogs I know personally I like m&m's Agent DiNozzo of Nele Kemena, m&m's Lector of Matty Williams, Marc Wagner's m&m's Biest and the dogs who stayed at our corporate kennel m&m's A'Kuba and m&m's Bonkers of family Menzel.

10) Hannibal is a tall, but also very slim dog. I do not know exact measurements but he will be easily above 70cm with a weight of around 31-33kg.

11) When Hannibal was round about one and a half years old I went to AVD e.V. summer event in 2014. It was the first time for me and the dog to put a foot on the dog field. It was Arne Pohlmeyer who offered the training and hosted the event and it was also the first time for me meeting up with him.

Hannibal was not firm with all the impressions, but I had the feeling that this freestyle sport was a thing he could be good in. The same day I also met a lot of people from the UK f.e. Satvinder Gill, Joe Griffith, Nathaniel Lewis and many more I am still in touch with today. Hannibal's and my own story is very simple. The first training was with Arne Pohlmeyer president of the club AVD e.V. and within the last 6 years I have become a member of the AVD e.V. and also a good friend of Arne Pohlmeyer.

I cannot imagine to join another club or do things differently therefore my club is and will be the AVD e.V. even it is a breeding club for presa canarios. I like to train with the other members like Alexander Menzel and Tobias Kraus, but I also have an eye for other clubs or a different way of working. I became also a good friend of members of De Vurige Herder, a NVDV club in Belgium and also of Peter Franck the head of De Heidehond in Gierle, Belgium.

These are all people/clubs where the focus of the work is not that much in scheme and where the gap is closed between common sports and security service dog work.

12) Hannibal's first step on a dog field was at the age of about one and a half years. I would have introduced him to work a way earlier if I had the chance to do it differently. Also Hannibal is my first dog and I made many mistakes as a first owner of dogs. But I am happy with him and also with all restrictions that come up with a dog like him within everyday life in a city I would not change one thing.

For sure Hannibal made me change doing many things differently with the dogs who followed him as I am also in a process of learning.

13) Hannibal is not social with people. Hannibal has to wear a muzzle in public since he was about six months old and he is always on leash. A dog like Hannibal cannot be handled in public without a lot of consideration and supervision.

14) After moving to a new home with a young Hannibal I wanted to introduce myself to the new neighbours and left the new flat for a few minutes.

Everything was already cleaned up and I have to mention that I am a huge collector of a lot of stuff like video games, comics, action figures. I left a 25kg bag of tile glue in the hallway and when I returned home there was just dust, dust, dust.

I think still today when I occupy myself with my collections then there is a bit of tile glue somewhere.

15) When I would change one thing it would not be Hannibal any more.

16) When Hannibal was young he tended to destroy a lot of stuff and he was also not social to people from the early beginning. I was not so firm in educating dogs but therefore I am very patient. I did maneuver him through these exciting times without a headache. I cannot say anything about his workability, because Hannibal was introduced to work/dogsport when he was an adult dog.

17) On the one hand Hannibal is a very relaxed and calm dog as long as he is in his familiar surroundings. He likes to hang around and is not the typical nervy dog who requests for activities or seems to be unbalanced if not worked. Primarily Hannibal is a companion dog or we can call him also a pet. He sleeps in bed, lies on the sofa, he eats pizza, pasta, everything.

Also my intention was to buy a companion dog as I had a light stroke at the age of 28 and I just wanted to force myself to be a bit more active while I have to go for walks with the dog and do other activities.

So the intention to become a dog owner was just to be a bit more active. The interest in working dogs and the fun in working the dogs had been a development after joining the first training at the AVD e.V. summer event in 2014. On the other hand Hannibal is a dog who is just devoted to me. There are very few people Hannibal accepts in his surrounding tending to just me.

18) I do not know Hannibal's litter mates. At the time of getting him I was not interested in names, parents, breeders, working and all other stuff I mostly now still do not have an eye for. I was just interested in a healthy dog. It was just possible to see Hannibal's parents from a distance outside the house, because I know now they were the same kind Hannibal is of.

19) Hannibal is social with all my other female dogs, another malinois Voodoo, a x-herder Dorie and a miniature bull terrier Peaches. Every dog on its own is also not uncomplicated, but Hannibal never had a problem with any of them. Instead of this Hannibal has got no contact with other dogs, to me it's also not necessary.

20) Hannibal lives in the house and he lives a typical petlife. I go out with him for walks, Hannibal is a raincoat owner and we do not take ourselves that seriously.

Dog 48 - Berry II (BRN13062)

Owner: Bert Lamers

Berry II is a dog with one of the most high quality offspring ever. A very social dog at home with extreme drives on the field. A dog who won the famous stud trial but unfortunately never got to trial because of several heavy injuries through his hard attacks.

Six littermates were titled. As a young dog, he was already something very special. Always very cool, willing to please, always want to work but very social. Bert Lamers trained him first (from 17 months), after that I trained him. He stayed with me till he passed away in May 2018.

He was a once in a lifetime dog, my BFF, an absolute legend! Very handsome and his weight was around 34 kg.

We trained together at many knpv clubs in the whole country.

He mated very many females and still does (artificial insemination) over the whole world , with excellent results .

273

Dog 49 - Ichi

Owner: Kieli Atherton

1. How is he / she at home, out of work?

When Ichi is not competing, he is your run of the mill pet. He has free rein of the house, does as he pleases and comes with me when I travel. Being my buddy was always first. Being a really great working dog was just an added bonus.

2. Describe his or her character with 5 words..

Intelligent, confident, happy, driven, loyal.

3. What is his / her best quality?

Ichi's best quality is his on/off switch. He is a monster in bitework and would turn it on at the drop of a dime if I needed him to in real life. But Ichi is also capable of being the sweetest, most gentle, loving dog with anyone. I think it is one of the things he is best known for in the PSA world. If I am at any Protection Sports Association event, without fail someone is going to ask me to get him out of the car so they can pet him. His demeanor is one of the things that has made his lines so popular. He offers the best of both worlds: a social, stable companion you can take anywhere, but will also not back down from a fight.

4. What is his / her least desirable attribute?

When it comes to a least desirable attribute there honestly is not a single thing that I do not love about this dog. It is why I call him the Unicorn. I truly could not have lucked out more when I adopted him as a puppy.

5. Is he / she one of your favourite dogs of all time?

Ichi is hands down the best dog I have ever owned. I have adored all my dogs, but Ichi and I balance each other out perfectly. Many times it was like he knew exactly what I needed from him before I even asked when out on the competition field.

6. What is his / her favourite activity?

His favorite activity is a toss up between people doting over him and biting decoys.

7. What is his / her biggest achievements?

Ichi has quite a few biggest achievements. Some of the most notable are: He is PSA's first handicap dog to reach a level 3. Placed 2nd at Nationals in the 1's, 2's and 3's. Took the high protection trophy at Nationals in the 2's and 3's. Awarded the highest score trophy for the level 2 competition season in 2016, and the level 3 competition season in 2018. He helped me become the first female to achieve 5 legs in the 3's. Along with being one of the most titled dogs in PSA history.

8. Was he / she difficult to train?

Ichi was difficult to train, just not in the way most people would think. Due to his birth defects he has breathing issues that makes it so he cannot have any pressure on his throat.

It instantly closes off his airways. This meant all collars of any type were not an option, excluding an extremely loose e-collar. Nearly everything had to be trained 100% reward based with really clear guidance. There was a lot of figuring out how to train behaviors in new ways that would work for him. Fortunately Ichi is a relativity compliant dog who values me as much as he enjoys working, so we were able to be successful. The process was not easy but it made me a better trainer and handler, which I am grateful for.

9. What's your favourite offspring of his / her?

Due to being born with a cleft palate he was neutered. I did not want to chance passing on his health issues.

10. How heavy was or is he / she?

In his prime, Ichi was about 60lbs.

11. Where is your training club and decoys who helped him / her?

We have been fortunate to train with almost every PSA club on the eastern seaboard here in the states. Some are still clubs, others are not. They know who they are and know I appreciate every single one of them. But the decoys who helped me lay most of his foundation in the beginning are Josh Knowlton, Steve Roberts and Nick Hodgen. Once we were working towards a PSA 3, Ichi and I trained a lot with Walter Quense.

12. If you have the same dog again, what will you so different?

If I had the same dog again I think I would start in the sport earlier. As a puppy Ichi had been shown foundation bitework, but then he was just a pet from the time he was a year until about the age of three. We did not start competing until he was four and a half years old. I think we could have achieved more than 5 legs in the 3's, but due to his age and the wear and tear this sport puts on a dog, I retired him before he sustained any long-term injuries. A dog as great as him deserves to be a healthy, happy old dog.

13. Is he / she social with people?

Ichi is amazing with people. I do not think he has ever met a person he did not like. He even adores children. So much so that I was once asked if Ichi could be part of a charity event that was a petting zoo for children. It quite possibly was the best day of his life.

14. Any funny stories you want to share?

Ichi unintentionally became a trend setter. As a puppy he started sitting up on his hind legs for attention. With his odd looking nose and small size he looked like a meerkat. So that became the term I used when he did it. He would randomly meerkat at competitions and spectators found it to be funny. People stated to teach their dogs the same behavior using meerkat as the cue, and now "meerkatting" is a thing.

15. If you can change 1 thing about the dog, what would it be?

I wouldn't change a single thing about him. He's perfect.

16. How was the dog like when he/ she as a puppy?

Ichi was such a good puppy. I really lucked out with him. From day one if he was not working, he was a laid back, easy-going guy.

17. How was he / she like as he / she matured?

As Ichi matured his personality never changed much. The only difference I ever saw was in his intensity towards decoys when he was in the fight with them. By the time we got to the point of competing he was out there with the intent to take them down.

18. How are the dog's litter mates?

Ichi has had more littermates make it to the 2's and 3's than any other line in the history of PSA. His father was the super accomplished PSA dog Zuko (Cartuck Van Joefarm). You'd be hard pressed to find a dog now in PSA that isn't in some way related to Ichi and his littermates from the Zuko x Isis breeding. After seeing how well these dogs performed everyone wanted one. Although I'd say Ichi is probably the most compliant and easy to work with of all the competition dogs from that breeding.

19. Is he / she social with other dogs?

Ichi is fantastic with other dogs. I work with dogs for a living and he has always been my go-to when addressing issues with client's dogs that are reactive or fearful of other dogs due to bad experiences. He is great at getting dogs to feel comfortable with dog to dog interaction again.

20. Does the dog live in a house or a kennel?

Ichi is a free-range house dog. He has never lived a day of his life as anything else.

Dog 50 - Blitzen

Owner: Ariel peldunas

1. How is he / she at home, out of work?

Out of drive, once mature, Blitzen was exactly what I wanted of a house/companion dog. She

had a wonderful off switch. I typically didn't even know where she was in the house. She would

alert and bark appropriately and was a good watchdog without being overly suspicious or

barking incessantly. She was clean and could be trusted to be loose in the house from aboul 1.5

years old and on. She was a great travel companion and was the type of dog that I could take anywhere without concern for her being a liability or acting out of control.

2. Describe his or her character with 5 words..

Versatile, intelligent, balanced, stoic, stable.

3. What is his / her best quality?

I would have to say Blitzen's intelligence was the major quality that contributed to everything else I admired about her. Once I learned how to best communicate with her, she acquired new

behaviors very quickly and was extremely versatile. She mastered everything I asked of her with relative ease and took new endeavors in stride as though she had been doing them her whole life. She kept me on my toes because she could figure out ways to get what she wanted without doing what I was asking, but I feel her intelligence forced me to become a better trainer because I had to make sure I was one step ahead of her.

4. What is his / her least desirable attribute?

Blitzen didn't have very good food drive until she was much older. She kind of worked for food

as though it was an obligation she wasn't happy about.

5. Is he / she one of your favourite dogs of all time?

It's hard to be objective about this, but I have raised and trained a lot of dogs and I feel Blitzen

exemplifies nearly all of the qualities I desire in working dogs. In addition, she was a wonderful

companion. Now that she's been gone a couple years, I do believe she's been my favorite dog to

both work and own.

6. What is his / her favourite activity?

Outside of biting, which I'm sure would be the favorite activity of most dogs trained in protection sports, Blitzen really did love to use her nose. I believe she enjoyed tracking/trailing immensely. As far as non-working activities, Blitzen loved to get attention from anyone she met and she also really seemed to enjoy hiking and swimming in the river.

7. What is his / her biggest achievements?

I believe most people who know Blitzen would list her achievements in PSA as her greatest

accomplishments. I would also put this at the top of the list. We earned a PSA 2 and PSA 3 in the same season, and took home the award for the highest overall score for both levels that year as well (2011). Blitzen had and may still have the highest obedience score for a dog in PSA 3.

Her scores were always very high and we took home many high obedience, high protection,

high owner trained, and high in trial awards. I think lesser known is, in addition to PSA, Blitzen and I traveled overseas to Iraq and Afghanistan to perform human remains detection for the US

military. Blitzen was an excellent human remains detection dog and tracking/trailing dog as well.

8. Was he / she difficult to train?

Early on, I struggled to maintain focus and engagement with Blitzen during obedience, especially around decoys and distractions. She also learned some bad habits during detection

and tracking work during the initial stages of training. Once I learned how to tap into her intelligence and allowed her to think and be more "operant", our relationship and performance

improved dramatically. So I would say, she was only difficult because I wasn't training smart enough. Once I learned to use my brain to engage hers, I found her to be a very easy dog to

train. I just needed to learn to speak her language.

9. What's your favourite offspring of his / her?

Unfortunately, Blitzen only had one litter and I've lost track of many of the puppies that were

eventually sold to police departments. Two are in sport homes and their owners have dabbled in

PSA to the extent they have been able and one was raised by a friend of mine as an active

companion. I was happy with their drives and temperaments (as were their owners), but it's

difficult to make an honest assessment without having more interaction and seeing the puppies

worked consistently.

10. How heavy was or is he / she?

Blitzen ranged from 50lbs in her younger years to about 65lbs when she matured. I tried to keep her around 55-60lbs when she was active and in shape.

11. Where is your training club and decoys who helped him / her?

Oh, I worked with so many different decoys and clubs on the east coast of the US, it truly was a team effort to prep her for PSA. I started her training when I worked at Tarheel K9 and would

travel back there from time to time for training and input from Jerry Bradshaw. Sean Siggins helped extensively with Blitzen's training for PSA. I worked quite a bit with Jeff Riccio as well.

Towards the later part of her PSA career, I trained more often with Rick Furrow, Nicole Hubert,

and Hillel Schwartzman.

12. If you have the same dog again, what will you so different?

If I could start over again with Blitzen as a puppy, I would start marker training immediately (I

didn't know much about it in 2005 when I brought her home) and I would be more fair during

training and communicating with her more effectively. I feel like she had to endure the struggles and confusion of me learning to train a lot of things for the first time and it makes me sad to

look back and think I put pressure on her at times for simply not understanding what I wanted.

13. Is he / she social with people?

Yes, very social with people.

14. Any funny stories you want to share?

Blitzen was a dog that made you feel stupid for laughing at her or making her do silly things. She always seemed so stoic and wise. However, I can think of a few times I did something stupid and she just took it in stride and looked at me disapprovingly. Once was when I was running with her at night when we were overseas and I tripped and fell over a speed bump. I managed to tuck and roll, get back up on my feet, and keep running. Blitzen just kept running at the same pace and I imagine when she looked over at me, if she could have shook her head, she would have. Another time, we were competing at the PSA Nationals and I tripped over a tarp during our obedience routine. Again, Blitzen just kept on heeling and maintained position while I struggled to stay upright. The funniest story I recall was during another PSA routine. I did my about turn too close to the cone and she stepped on it. As we were heeling back, I noticed a strange noise and Blitzen's gait seemed awkward out of the corner of my eye but she was still in position giving me attention. About halfway back, the judge told me to halt where there wasn't usually a halt. Once I stopped, I was told to remove the cone from my dog's leg. I looked down and Blitzen was sitting there in heel position with a traffic cone halfway up her back leg. When she stepped on it, it got stuck on her, but instead of being upset or distracted, she just kept heeling on three legs. I feel those stories really illustrate so much about her personality and work ethic.

15. If you can change 1 thing about the dog, what would it be?

If I could change anything overall, I wish Blitzen could have been a bit more affectionate with

me. She was always so independent, even as a puppy. She loved attention from anyone else, but

was more reserved with me. In the work, if I could change something, I would have liked her to

have a more naturally full, pushing grip. Her grip was not bad and she learned to push, but she wasn't really possessive and didn't naturally want to swallow the sleeve or wrap her legs.

16. How was the dog like when he/ she as a puppy?

Blitzen never really acted like a puppy. She always seemed like an adult dog in a puppy's

body, intense; independent; pushy; had a civil edge during bite training; more of a serious worker than happy-go-lucky, silly puppy.

17. How was he / she like as he / she matured?

As an adult, Blitzen was the type of dog that took everything in stride and just had a wise, "been

there-done that" attitude. Still had an intense, civil edge during bite work but she was well balanced; very social and stable; strong work ethic in all aspects of training; her temperament was excellent and she was a dog that I would trust around anyone, adults or children.

18. How are the dog's litter mates?

I don't know much about any of her littermates. Her breeder kept back a male and said he was a very nice dog. He was used as a stud dog a number of times.

19. Is he / she social with other dogs?

Social, but pushy and assertive/dominant with unfamiliar dogs.

20. Does the dog live in a house or a kennel?

She lived in the house, sometimes crated, sometimes loose in the earlier part of her life and then loose once she was retired around 7-8.

Dog 51 - Ashley vom Clan der Wölfe
(VDH/DMC10/0032)

Owner: Oliver Schilling

Ashley came to see me Easter 2010. Since then she always lived with me during the day in a kennel in the evening with me in the house. She was very uncomplicated and the only thing she always wanted was to be near me. As long as she can see me, she stays in her place, she doesn't see me anymore, she runs after me. Dealing with visitors was often unproblematic because she is not interested in other people and ignores them. Only one may not touch her if she does not want to do so she shows this relatively fast and consequently. Something different was this when my son was born, he is also ignored unless he has something edible in his hand, but a stranger was not allowed to approach the baby carriage. It was very interesting that Ashley got a milk shot immediately after we got back from the hospital and wanted to help take care of my son. Even if these two do not have a loving relationship until today, she is always close to him when he goes for a walk and is the best bodyguard in the world!

Sportingly Ashley was not always an easy dog. She often made it difficult for me during training and sometimes we had a difference of opinion which was not always discussed without a fight. It took me a while to understand you. It was never her need to run after a ball, her motivation was to bite into something to be able to argue with me. She had very little prey, which in subordination always made it a little difficult to train. In the tracking and protection service I never had problems with her. If she was young again today I would like to build up the subordination a little bit differently.

Our biggest success was the victory of the DMC Championship 2018 as the oldest dog with 8 years and 3 months and our 8th place on the FMBB World Championship 2019 with 9 years. I was especially proud that she gave everything in the final and in b and c she made 4 points miore than in the World Cup and took home the cup for the best track of the World Championship. Of course, this would not have been possible without any help. We have a great training team with e.g. Marc Oliver Radke (multiple participant of the FMBB/FCI World Championship with his dog Ferro du Mont st. Aubert or Jörg Schwabe German Champion ADRK with Boss vom Kriegsdamm and helper FMBB WM in Germany)including all the others who have also participated in German championships. The special thing about it is that we are not a club or a team but all friends who do a lot together in private!

During our sporting career from 2013 to 2019 we had 4 litters with a total of 28 puppies. The first two were via Antrax Ostraryka, the other 2 via service dogs of the police Margaux du Mont st. Aubert and Xach of Kraft Hill. I am very proud that all offspring are healthy and there are no dental defects. Some of them were already twisted at national and international championships and have already produced offspring themselves, e.g. Destiny, Daiquiri and Doctor vom Hirtengarten (Ashley X Antrax). Ashley's offspring are also welcome in service. The police officers are very happy about their dogs.

Ashley is not one of the best sport dogs for me - there are certainly others, but in general she is one of the best of this generation for me. She has heart courage, a lot of aggression and she was the best mother in the world! I hope that our offspring Elena will be as good as her mother. And there I am not talking about points on the course but about a quality dog that is hardly available today. Ashley was it no matter if this one had a protection arm, full protection or nothing on if this person was the enemy he was bitten too!

Even at 10 years old you still have to look after her a bit even if her needs have changed. She likes to go swimming or lie around in the sun and wait for her meals. From time to time we look for a track and she sometimes strains her head but otherwise we enjoy our life in the pension.

Dog 52 – Branco (BRN22727)

Owner: Marcel Alders and Emily Houk

This excerpt will be the recollections and current experiences of owning Branco through Marcel Aalders. I, Emily Houk, will just be putting it on paper, as according to Marcel I speak just a tad bit more eloquently than him. Further, Branco did not come into my life until he was 7 years old. Thus, a fuller report of the entirety of the dog is better suited to be explained through Marcel.

Branco was out of the combination of Dax x Noa, born on May 1, 2012. Branco was bred by John te Lindert, and John also owned and raised Branco until he was about 15 months. I can not comment much as to how Branco was as a young dog under 15 months, aside from the couple times I saw him as a younger dog training with John. From the few glimpses I saw of him before I got him, he was as much a pain in the ass then, as he was once I bought him around 15 months old.

Branco is a very black and white dog. He requires a lot of clarity, and he's not the type of dog you can fool around with. Emily often, even now will try to rough house with him, and he will go from 0 to biting the hell out of you in a second. He is just playing, but doesn't realize how hard he bites.

Branco is also a dominant type. His biggest issue in training was always his stubbornness. The harder you went on him, the harder he would fight back. He is a completely social dog outside of work, but in work, as soon as you put pressure on him he fights back. He is a very hard dog as well, and that made training him difficult.

He is quite possessive as well. He hunts well, but it's more out of possession then it is actual desire to search. This also caused a problem on the box. He always wanted to grab it out of possession/ frustration which eventually led to him ripping a canine out on the box. I made the mistake of trying to replace it with a titanium tooth. After several weeks, he returned back to training and ended up just ripping out the titanium tooth as well.

For me, Branco has been a great stud. He produces well over different types of females, and his traits still come through strong even in an outcross. He has many offspring that are working in police all over the world, as well as military. He also has several offspring competing in different sports, as well as within the KNPV program. He has also been DNA tested through two different companies and was medically 100%, including of course x rays.

I believe Branco's most notable siblings would be Dino Lindert and Biko Abbink. They all seem to exhibit similar traits as well as produce similarly.

Outside of work Branco is very social and laid back. He goes along with other dogs, people, even cats. I think like Dax, if people saw him in normal life they wouldn't think the dog was much of anything.

Dog 53 – Kuno (BRN18465)

Owner: Bart Roosen

1. How is he / she at home, out of work?

Very nice dog to have with you.

2. Describe his or her character with 5 words..

Very nice, good character, always happy.

3. What is his / her best quality?

Very hard push bite

4. What is his / her least desirable attribute?

Jump exercises he did not like

5. Is he / she one of your favourite dogs of all time?

Very nice dog handling.

6. What is his / her favourite activity?

Posing and eating.

7. What is his / her biggest achievements?

Judging knpv 424 points game 430 points.

8. Was he / she difficult to train?

Start easy dog but then a little older he got harder.

9. What's your favourite offspring of his / her?

A son of Kuno.

10. How heavy was or is he / she?

35 kilograms.

11. Where is your training club and decoys who helped him / her?

In Tilburg the persistence of the helper members of the club.

12. If you have the same dog again, what will you so different?

The same.

13. Is he / she social with people?

Social for everyone.

14. Any funny stories you want to share?

I do not change anything, he is perfect.

15. If you can change 1 thing about the dog, what would it be?

Quiet studious puppy.

16. How was the dog like when he/ she as a puppy?

Very fine almost remained the same.

17. How was he / she like as he / she matured?

Social to other dogs.

18. How are the dog's litter mates?

Brothers are not the same line. All good resembling real Kunos.

19. Is he / she social with other dogs?

Funny story, call back couples of times he really did not like it he also showed he was not funny.

20. Does the dog live in a house or a kennel?

He is always in the kennel.

Dog 54 - Churchmount Jurko (LOSH91592452)

Owner: Joeri Vanheuckelom

Jurko is always ready for action at any time. When he is at home and nothing is happening around him, he is calm. It is not a nervous dog. He is watchful and our property is also his property. Strange people and strange dogs are not allowed around him, but it's not in an aggressive way. It is his dominant character that emerges the watchfulness.

His character in 5 words: Champion, dominant, honest, drives, excellent bite.

His best qualities are his natural hard grip, always pushing and crushing. The least attributes are keeping him satisfied in work and keeping his high drives under control.

For sure, he is my favourite dog I ever owned and trained. We wrote history together and he will always have a special place in my heart.

Difficult to say what his favourite thing is to do. Retrieving, biking, hiking, biting or protection work, it is all on his top list. A special note maybe, when he is in breeding modus, he allows all females and the owners, he stays focused on the female and never minds the rest.

He wrote history in NVBK ring sport. 3 times champion in a row, in 3 different categories:

Champion category 3 2017 + Top of the ranking Champion category 2 2018 + Top of the ranking (best dog of the year in the category)

Champion category 1 2019 + Provincial champion of Antwerp

He is a very smart dog, but with his strong and dominant character and high drives he needs an experienced trainer. Daily exercises to keep boundaries and control.

It is difficult to choose a favourite son or daughter of Jurko. He bred many different females and his offspring are participating in many sports or are working for customs. I am proud of all of them and appreciate the contact with the breeders and becoming friends.

10) Through the years, many people have helped us. Many decoys and helpers, on and beside the training field played a big role to become a multi champion. Also, my family had an important role in the achievements.

If I could have the same dog again, I would not change a thing. It would be a blessing to have a son after him who is a copy of his dad. I must admit, it will not be easy for any dog to come in line with Jurko for me. The time and energy I put in him; it was all worth it.

In his younger years, even when he was a little puppy, he did not give ground for anything. A puppy, stable in his head and mind, good in any environment and a big urge to possess objects. So, when I look at Jurko now as an adult and fully trained dog, I will look again for these qualities in a future puppy.

Churchmount Jurko

Churchmount Jurko

Churchmount Jurko

Dog 55 – Bomber (BRN33926)

Owner: Michael John Hutchinson

1. How is he / she at home, out of work?

Bomber when he was younger was a bit of a nightmare as a pup. I can remember the day I got Bomber; he had travelled over 16 hours to my house along with his siblings from the breeder Graham Orielly 'Ireland working k9' I bought him from. As soon as he entered my backyard, he was bouncing around like he'd been there all his life, compared to his siblings. Within days of playing with him and doing things with him I just knew he was the pup I'd been searching for. In his younger days he was a bit of a handful, he wanted everyone and anything that came in our house or if we were outside, he would scream to be at them. Then when I started channelling in to work, I could see that I had a good puppy on my hands, and then doing environmental work with him, getting him out and about to different places and environments nothing phased Bomber at all.

2. Describe his or her character with 5 words..

Bomber is very much strong headed, confident, eager, no self-respect for himself. He has a very strong demeanor about himself. Nothing phases him at all, I've taken him round the country working on numerous training grounds with numerous decoys and all his characteristics shine through from him anywhere in any place.

3. What is his / her best quality?

His best quality would have to be his self-assurance, he is very sure of himself. He just thinks he's unstoppable and invincible. He is always ready for work any place, anywhere. His best quality in a nutshell would be that he 'does not care '

4. What is his / her least desirable attribute?

His 6' o clock morning wake up calls, making sure he's heard and wakes the full house up, he will not do his business in his crate or kennel. He won't stop barking till we let him out. The first thing he does when I open that crate is jump up, licks my face and gives me the odd head butt.

5. Is he / she one of your favourite dogs of all time?

Yes, he's the best dog I've owned to date, and to be honest I don't think I'll ever get a one as good as Bomber again in my life. He really is something special. The biggest thing for me in these working dogs is what they are like in the real world out of drive. Many of the ones I've had in the past have failed in the real-world scenarios. I can take Bomber anywhere, any place whether it's day or night, snow or rain he shows up and does what he does best. He has never failed me, and that for me is all I want in a dog.

6. What is his / her favourite activity?

His favourite activity is coming out on long walks with me daily, and he loves chasing rabbits and hares with my other dogs.

7. What is his / her biggest achievements?

His biggest achievement for me was when I entered him into the AVD puppy class night trials, he was 7 months old. Of the 36 dogs in the competition, Bomber came 1st place. He absolutely smashed it. I've never won a thing in my life, so this achievement is the one thing that will stick with me forever. His trophies' is a nice reminder of his success. He has also won 2nd place silver class, and 2nd place long send suit. Bomber to date has entered 3 trials winning 5 trophies.

8. Was he / she difficult to train?

From day 1 Bomber had a great desire to bite. He does do obedience, but he's not overall fussed about it as it's not his strongest point. He isn't overall fussed about searching, which I'm not either. He makes up for all this in his bite work. My whole purpose for Bomber was to be a trial dog, but more importantly a personal protection dog, and for me to work security with him for my line of work.

9. What's your favourite offspring of his / her?

So far all of Bombers offspring are young, but what I have seen from the litter I personally bred from a bitch of mine to him I really liked everything about his pups. They all had a great desire to bite, from a young age they were calm on the bite, they were very possessive on the bite which was just naturally in them. I've seen about 4 pups out of that litter work and they all have great drive, and such a calming demeanor on the bite just like their dad. It's what I like to see in puppies, and it's a nice thing to see him passing on his traits.

10. How heavy was or is he / she?

Bomber is just over 40kg in weight, and he is 26 ½ inches to the shoulder. He is very thick set for his breed, with a very good strong head on top of his very awesome set of shoulders.

11. Where is your training club and decoys who helped him / her?

I've never had just one club that I train at, I like to travel around to different clubs around the UK. So, I can work my dogs on different decoys and different environments. I believe it makes a good strong dog, but that's just my opinion.

12. If you have the same dog again, what will you so different?

If I was to own the same dog again, I would train the out command from young. I think I would add more control to him but saying that the way he is now he fits in with my lifestyle. But a bit more control and an out command wouldn't go a miss.

13. Is he / she social with people?

Bomber isn't a very sociable dog, but he will tolerate people to some extent. If anyone comes up close to me, he will react to them straight away. He absolutely loves his family though, especially my kids.

14. Any funny stories you want to share?

Bomber is very lucky he never lost his life this day, but it is funny now looking back. When I walked him on an abandoned tip, he decided it would be fun to run and attack a big HGV truck. He started running after it then he kept attacking the wheels as it was moving. Then he suddenly locked into the wheel, causing the wheel to flip him over. He ended up under the truck, I'm running behind frantic screaming for the driver to stop. The driver finally stopped, then Bomber the lorry driver and started pouncing up to his high cab door. The man went to get out of his truck to give Bomber a stroke, I had to push the man back in his truck and tell him Bomber had other intentions and being his friend certainly wasn't one of them.

15. If you can change 1 thing about the dog, what would it be?

N/A.

16. How was the dog like when he/ she as a puppy?

Bomber as a puppy was hard work, very reactive towards people from day one. He just wanted to be with me all the time. I knew I had found a good dog to build on, and these traits I could use for his further training.

17. How was he / she like as he / she matured?

Bomber has now matured into a nice balanced dog that fits into mine and my family's lifestyle. He just wants to chill, and that's the type of dog I like. Until he's given the command to work then he changes.

18. How are the dog's litter mates?

To be fair there were only four in Bomber's litter, there were 3 males and 1 female. I only know of the female being worked, I haven't seen anything of the males so I couldn't comment on them.

19. Is he / she social with other dogs?

I've got two other dogs myself; he absolutely loves them, they're his friends. But out on the lead he can be dog reactive, but within 5 minutes I can have him running around with the same dog.

20. Does the dog live in a house or a kennel?

80% of the time he lives in the house with me, my partner and children. But he would live in or out not a problem.

Dog 56 – Spartan (BRN32026)

Owner: Stephen Simmonds

Spartan is a very well known dog in the 'doggy world'. He is a pleasure, easy to live with and a quiet happy dog. Great with my kids and my wife and has no interest in other dogs. He is quite happy to be in the kennels or lying on the living room floor.

He is calm, chilled, loving, obedient but also a very serious dog when he needs to be. When he is in 'work mode' he is fast on his feet, hits hard, intent and has a natural full hard grip but also an all round level headed dog.

Just one of his best qualities must be his ability to switch on with serious drive and intent but also to switch off turning into a big softy.

He is by far the best dog I have ever owned. His confidence and focus is second to none. I've had a few dogs now and none come close to 'SuperSpartan'!

His favourite activity is definitely 'bite work'. He gets so hyped up for it and loves whatever you throw at him, he works at his best when under pressure.

Being such a versatile dog he adjusts to things very quickly, he has a list of achievements starting from a young age, Lorockmor Defend & Pursue Puppy 1st, Halloween Charity Trials-puppy class 2nd, Lorockmor Defend & Pursue Level 1 1st, Lorockmor Defend & pursue Level 2 1st (2 years running), Halloween Charity Trials suit class 2nd, ZWP1 & 2, ADV Night Trials Silver Class 4th, Clash of Courage 2nd, NASDU Level 2, E.C.A Fight or Flight Intermediate 1st plus Long Send 2nd. This just shows how adaptable and serious this dog is.

We are based in Northern Ireland, our club is a close knit family of no more than 6 members. Our main decoy, Martin McCullough has helped us endlessly, also Alan Young, Billy Wilkinson and Dusty Johnston have all helped and been on the journey alongside Spartan and myself. #teamwork We also make regular trips to BVK, Scott and Chloe which is home from home for us.

If I had the same dog all over again, I'd do everything the exact same way. I wouldn't change a thing about him. Spartan's work ethic is off the chart but when he is 'switched off' he is very social with people and other dogs, you can walk him through the park or through the middle of a busy town with no fear or worries of him biting or showing any type of aggression.

Funny story- Billy Wilkinson and I took our dogs to the beach, Spartan is obsessed with water he loves swimming, I had him on a long line in a down position beside me just taking in the scenery when Billy threw a ball for his own dog and Spartan took off after it, me not knowing the long line was wrapped around my leg. I ended up 3 feet in the air and dragged down the beach!

I wouldn't change a thing about Spartan, I love his craziness and his calm gentle nature.

Unfortunately I can't comment on what Spartan was like as a puppy. As much as I would love to take full credit for the amazing dog he has turned into, I have to give credit where credit is due, Ash Fielding played a massive part in Spartans training as a pup. He built Spartan up imprinting him and putting great foundations into him making him the dog he is today, strong, confident and clear.

He mainly lives outside in kennels however i do sneak him in the house for a cuddle when the wife isn't in (Don't tell the wife)!

Dog 57 - Doc Vom Zeitzerland (VDH/DMC06/347)

Owner: Danny Lines

1. How is he / she at home, out of work?

Doc was mainly a kennel dog although he did spend time indoors but created havoc.

2. Describe his or her character with 5 words..

Strong, civil, loving, powerful and happy.

3. What is his / her best quality?

Civilian work - natural aggression.

4. What is his / her least desirable attribute?

Mischievous.

5. Is he / she one of your favourite dogs of all time?

Yes it would be hard to find another like him.

6. What is his / her favourite activity?

Man work (biting).

7. What is his / her biggest achievements?

Ipo3 with two national championships, bringing in various tv series including sky one - A Different Breed and Waiting as a parks police dog.

8. Was he / she difficult to train?

Yes he was difficult as he was predominantly a police or security dog and to train him it was difficult to turn the aggression into a high level sports dog.

9. What's your favourite offspring of his / her?

There are so many, he had over 100 studs in civilian, security and police. It would be difficult to choose, although one in particular springs to mind Rod Dunn's female that went to the world championships a few times.

10. How heavy was or is he / she?

He weighed around 42kg

11. Where is your training club and decoys who helped him / her?

Our club is Britannia K9 Security in Essex, but myself and Doc were trained mainly in Germany and Belgium. I used many different decoys from the UK and Europe. They all did amazing things with him and they all know who they are.

12. If you have the same dog again, what will you so different?

I wouldn't do anything different with Doc, he was perfect in every way. The only flaw he had was tracking, I would have taught that differently to him.

13. Is he / she social with people?

I liked him to be under control but not too social as he was working on the streets.

14. Any funny stories you want to share?

Whilst filming sky ones "A Different Breed" we did a scene where Doc had a dubbed Belgian voice pretending to talk to me and during filming doc farted so loud and everyone on set rolled around laughing. They kept it in the documentary as it was too funny not to include it.

15. If you can change 1 thing about the dog, what would it be?

From him to have recovered from an injury he sustained doing operational work that put him into retirement from competition. That was a sad day

16. How was the dog like when he/ she as a puppy?

I bought him when he was 10 months old as a green young dog. As a puppy he lived in a family home.

17. How was he / she like as he / she matured?

He was a very strong dog and would take a lot of pressure, was very suspicious and had super defence but great nerve.

18. How are the dog's litter mates?

All of his litter mates made sport and police dogs.

19. Is he / she social with other dogs?

Doc was very social with other dogs.

20. Does the dog live in a house or a kennel?

He lived in a kennel his entire life.

Dog 58 - Bouiz ùdoli Jizery (ČMKU BOM/6553/13/18)

Owner: Tomáš loud

1) How is home, without work?

Bouí is such a family dog, he is our friend. He is not in conflict and can tolerate other dogs in the household. He absolutely loves people and I don't have to be afraid to leave him alone with the children.

2) Describe his character in 5 words.

Hardworking, tireless, social, guardian and personality.

3) What is his best quality?

He is balanced and can work in peace, which pays off on odor work. He has had very intense tracking since he was a child and solves problems in peace. It can be said that the harder the terrain, the more they try.

4) What is his least desirable attribute?

He is quite possessive and is guarding his place. Whether at home in a pen or transport trolley. He really looks bad here. We have clearly set the rules that must be followed. In any case, he never really bit anyone.

5) Is he one of your favorite dogs of all time?

He is my number one so far and it's possible it will stay that way. But every dog I raced with had a top and in a way was my number one. In any case, we have the greatest success so far with Boui.

6) What is his favorite activity?

He probably enjoys everything the same way. As for the disciplines, he certainly doesn't have one that wouldn't please him. When it comes to free time, we like to ride a bike, or he likes swimming or frisbee.

7) What are his greatest achievements?

Probably winning the CACIT in Dobříš. Or 2nd place at MR BOM CR, where we had the same number of points as the dog in 1st place and decided up to 1 point on defense. Of course, a huge success for us was 2x 5th place in the basic part of FMBB.

8) Was he difficult to train?

Bouí was not a completely simple dog and we made many mistakes that haunt us to this day. But over time, we sat down and training became a toy for us.

9) What is your favorite offspring?

In our country, Bouí is very related. That's why he doesn't have many children. But I have his son at home and a friend's brother both have great potential. It's Extreme Bouí and Ektor from kennel Rebell Represent.

10) How heavy was he?

N/A.

11) Where is your training club and who helped him?

I train in the club ZKO Žd'árek, which is run under the Czech Kennel Club. I really have many friends who help me with the training and it would be a long list who has ever helped us.

12) If you have the same dog again, what will be so different for you?

The extreme is not so different from Boui, they are different in some ways, but he has a lot of things after his father. The difference is in the training methods that have undergone development during that time, and most importantly, one has to adapt to the change of test rules and the requirements of the judges themselves.

13) Is he social with people?

Absolutely, Bouí loves people. When he can cuddle with someone, he is the happiest dog under the sun.

14) Any funny stories you want to share?

We once had a team built on Cacit. A friend who was on our team started the trail and in the course his dog urinated. This, of course, led to our funny allusions. We had a little fun with that. The next day, Boui and I followed the trail. After about 20 meters, the dog hunched over and did the deed. Since then, I know that karma is free and I prefer not to joke about anything. I have to add, however, that Bouí really had intestinal problems and even after the corresponding point loss, we were able to win.

15) If you can change 1 thing about a dog, what would it be?

I wouldn't change anything.

16) What was he like when he was a puppy?

He had a huge appetite. It took Boui longer to show his hunting instincts, but then he became a great predator, somewhere around 1 year of age.

17) How is he like as he matures?

His adolescence was no problem.

18) How are his littermates?

Boui's siblings are also very successful. If I'm not mistaken, there were 9 of them in the litter. Of these, 7 individuals competed at the top level. One as a specialist in customs.

19) Is he social with other dogs?

He is non-conflicting, works at home with other dogs and has never provoked any battle. But he can only be provoked to play with another dog if he wants to.

20) Does the dog live in a house or kennel?

With us, dogs have their space and we also have our space. So the dogs are in pens.

Dog 59 – Keizer (BRN27949)

Owner: David Campbell

Keizers accomplishments and achievements:
- 3 successful litters - children competing at championship levels.
- LWD Dogs - 2nd place level 1.
- Certified PSA PDC Dog.
- PSA 1 Titled Dog (first in Europe).
- 2018 AVD Gold Class - 2nd place.
- ZWP - Pass
- Starred in Line Of Duty (BBC Drama).
- PSA Decoy Dog - Successful break down of decoys.

Going back to when I was a young boy at the age of 7, dogs have been a massive part of my life. Around 8 years ago I came across a dog breed I had never experienced before; Belgian Malinois. This was a whole new ballgame for me but with a lot of research about this breed I jumped in feet first and purchased my first malinois ' Keizer '. I travelled to Dublin and bought Keizer at a reasonable price of €500 Euros, this is where our journey in the dog world really began for us. From only weeks old Keizer's potential was unbelievable, he ticked every box in my book. As the weeks went in Keizer and I became inseparable, he was like my sidekick.

Here in Northern Ireland at the time I first started my journey with Keizer there was only one dog club accessible to train this sort of breed. So I joined the IPO club and paid roughly £200 for the year and £5.00 every week towards training and equipment costs at the club. After a few months I came to the conclusion that this club simply was not right for me or Keizer. Back to the drawing board of where I could go to train my dog, I finally came across another dog club in Belfast. This club was very different to the previous club I tried so I was intrigued to give it a go. While training at this dog club I was introduced to a few boys who had the exact same mindset I had of where I wanted to progress training Keizer, and from that moment K9NI was created.

In the beginning we trained with our own equipment in my back garden, we could see a big development in our dogs and decided to put our dogs training to the test, so we travelled overseas to England for our team to compete in 'Lorockmor Dogs'. This event unfolded over 2 days and was a big test for the team as it was our first dog event as K9Ni. Keizer competed in Level 1 and finished in 2nd place, this really gave us the encouragement that our training was paying off.

Our first event gave us massive determination to push our dogs further up the scale of training. We entered our 2nd event 'The 2018 AVD 5K9 Event' in England known as the ultimate test and challenge for working dogs. I had never experienced an event like this one before, I was mesmerised watching other dogs compete in this event. The time came for Keizer to compete, he was competing in the 'Gold Class'. I remember feeling a whole lot of different emotions but I was very confident and excited because I knew Keizer would smash my expectations.

My attitude and motto I portrayed to Keizer was to have fun and enjoy every minute. I believe to this day Keizer was made for these challenges as every test he was up against he powered through them. The moment came where we found out Keizer's results and to my surprise and delight he came 2nd place! This was a big achievement for us as this event has very impressive dogs competing in it.

Another big encouragement for our team, we then started a new journey with PSA DogSport as Keizer was already a certified PSA PDC dog. Our next challenge to overcome was 'PSA Title One'. We brought our American friends and PSA family over to trial with us on our home soil. We held the trials over 2 days, first day covered the obedience aspect and second day covered protection.

Keizer passed his obedience with a couple of points to spare and smashed his protection, I knew by Keizer's attitude that day that he was going to succeed in the protection aspect of the event. All our hard work has paid off as Keizer became the first PSA title dog in Europe. The feeling of achievement was surreal, as any dog man would know it's not often you get a dog that has it all.

Keizer was the backbone of my family and the K9NI family. He could never be replaced in my eyes. I lost a piece of myself when I lost him. He is the reason I began and lived this journey and he will be sorely missed forever. Keizer passed in December 2019, he rests at home with us where he belongs.

I would like to show my gratitude to all the K9Ni family, old and new. K9Ni supported and encouraged Keizer and I every step of the way on our journey.

Dog 60 – Rowdy (BRN29908)

Owner: Billy Wilkinson

1. How is he / she at home, out of work?

Rowdy is a fantastic bitch at home, very social with family and friends. But will let you know if a stranger is about. I have a 6 year old boy with autism and she is fantastic with him. She will lie down by his side during the day and follow him everywhere.

2. Describe his or her character with 5 words..

Drivey, athletic, stable, loyal and fun.

3. What is his / her best quality?

I would say Rowdy's best quality is that she is very clear. When we are working she is nasty with intent and at home she is a social dog.

4. What is his / her least desirable attribute?

Rowdy's least desirable attribute is that you couldn't take your eyes off her in the house if she gets 5 minutes on her own she will get up to all sorts of mischief. Chewing things, lifting things and destroying them, typical Mali.

5. Is he / she one of your favourite dogs of all time?

Yes, I got Rowdy after a 7 hour round trip at 6 week old and from then she very rarely leaves my side. She goes to work with me most days and always accompanies me when I go anywhere in the van.

6. What is his / her favourite activity?

6) Rowdy's favourite activity has to be bite work. She will work for hours and never gets bored of it.

7. What is his / her biggest achievements?

Rowdy earned her PSA 1 title 2018 she is one of only 3 females in europe to have this title.

She passed her ZWPI & ZWP2 in 2018

She has completed Bronz & silver at the AVDs.

She was 1st in the obedience at the AVDs in 2019.

Came first in the long send competition in august 2019.

Came 2nd in the intermediate trial.

8. Was he / she difficult to train?

Rowdy is a high drive bitch and as a puppy she was hard to out, it was my fault. I left it too long to teach her the out and she was a year old and we had a lot of conflict at the time but we got there in the end.

9. What's your favourite offspring of his / her?

My favourite offspring is Ivy owned by Stephen Simmonds, her drive is through the roof, a very confident bitch and just takes everything that's thrown at her.

I train with her very week so I see the progress

To be far all the puppies out of her litter are doing very well with their new handlers I have high expectations of these pups

10. How heavy was or is he / she?

Rowdy always sits around 36kg. She is a very big bitch with heavy bone but very athletic and always gets mistaken for a male.

11. Where is your training club and decoys who helped him / her?

Our training club is Urban Street dogs N.Ireland based in Co Antrim.

Rowdy has worked with a lot of decoys over the years in her early years most of her training was done with Alan Young of Spiers K9 who I still regularly train with.

Our club decoy is Martin McCulloch who week in week out puts Rowdy through her paces.

I have also worked with my family over the pond Scott Bullvision who I visit regularly as well as Rodney Stoute in my early years helped me alot and Rockel Lewis.

12. If you have the same dog again, what will you so different?

If I had the same dog again I would definitely have taught her the out a lot earlier and done more obedience at an earlier age.

We hear a lot of people say obedience too young brings the dogs drive down. They are very wrong if you have a very high drive dog obedience will help them be more stable.

13. Is he / she social with people?

Rowdy is a very social bitch when me or my wife are about, I can have friends and their children come visit with no problems at all.

14. Any funny stories you want to share?

I have many funny stories, most of which put me in the bad books with the wife. I fell asleep one night watching the UFC in the early hours and was woke by the wife shouting "See that fucking dog!!"

Rowdy had gone up the stairs, lifted her hair products and proceeded to chew them to pieces on the spare bed.

On another occasion Rowdy was out outside eating her food and I heard them words again from the wife "See that fucking dog!" I jumped up, there was a box of Budweiser sitting at the back door and she had taken the caps of 6 bottles and was lapping the bear coming out.

15. If you can change 1 thing about the dog, what would it be?

To be honest I wouldn't change a thing. She's a very well rounded bitch and will take on anything I ask her to do.

16. How was the dog like when he/ she as a puppy?

She was a very confident little pup, just loved to work and learned very quickly.

17. How was he / she like as he / she matured?

Rowdy got better with age; she definitely hasn't slowed down in the work department.

But she is a lot more easy to live with now as she lives in the house and is a lot more settled. Instead of the crazy mali we all have to deal with.

18. How are the dog's litter mates?

I only know of one of her litter mates owned by Phil Lockhart, amale dog working in the security industry. He's very like Rowdy.

19. Is he / she social with other dogs?

Rowdy is very social with other dogs as are all the dogs I keep, she will play with any dog and can be very full on to most dogs.

My friend Kenny Thomas has a working terrier and he said that was the only dog he ever saw that tired him out.

20. Does the dog live in a house or a kennel?

Rowdy did live outside in a kennel for a while. But after she had her pups we decided to keep her in the house from now on.

Dog 61 - Campari vom clan der Wolfe
(CKC1141834)

Owner: Christine Kisser

Flew to Vancouver, BC from Frankfurt January 2, 2014

1. How is he / she at home, out of work?

What shocked me the most about Campari from the first day he stepped into his new home at 10 weeks old was that he immediately found a red pillow on the floor , laid on and watched me for a very long time. He was immediately calm. I had GSD's for 20 years prior and none of them were ever that calm at 10 weeks old, never mind 10 months old. Campari has a SERIOUS off switch. He loves to lay down and relax, you'll forget he's even there because his breathing is so silent. He will light up to a knock or noise but he is not an active barker at home, more of a one occasional bark and a very low growl with a cobra snake tail. He is stable, calm and serious.

2. Describe his or her character with 5 words..

He is stable, calm, serious, loyal and a fighter.

3. What is his / her best quality?

This is a difficult question because he has many amazing qualities however I would have to say his calm serious nature makes him a pleasure to be around.

4. What is his / her least desirable attribute?

He is not reactive at all and needs to be activated through active shaping exercises and frustration, not through active force. This can be a difficult dog for some people because he could show handler sensitivity and lose his happy picture.

5. Is he / she one of your favourite dogs of all time?

He is my favorite dog of all time. I would not change one thing about him.

6. What is his / her favourite activity?

'Jack' loves to swim after sticks, play fight with me (he recently dislocated my finger while play fighting) and real fight with the decoy.

7. What is his / her biggest achievements?

We were listed as Top Dog in Canada in 2018 by the GSSCC (German Shepherd Dog Club of Canada). Highest Points in Tracking, Obedience and Protection, 4th Place World Championships for Malinois FMBB 2019, 5th Place Final Qualifier FMBB 2019, Winner USA Nationals October 2019, Qualified for FMBB 2020 World Championship Canadian Team however cancelled due to Covid19.

8. Was he / she difficult to train?

Yes in the first 18 months he was difficult to train because he easily showed handler sensitivities to my 'old school training methods' I had to learn new ways to train this type of dog. It was however a fantastic learning experience for me as a handler of 18 years in IPO- learning to change my training.

9. What's your favourite offspring of his / her?

Once again a very difficult question to answer: I have kept two females from his C litter, I like their balance. Bred to a fiery female Mecberger Suka. Josh Markow in the USA is showing beautiful work with a beautiful offspring of his. D'Zero Malinois God of War Kennel, Michael Mengers Fireballs B litter Bodhi is also showing really nice work thus far. I'm excited to see all of them show to their best and live a fantastic life as part of the family.

10. How heavy was or is he / she?

Jack is approximately 78-85lbs in range depending on the season.

11. Where is your training club and decoys who helped him / her?

I resigned from clubs in 2014 for a variety of reasons that would be very politically incorrect to talk about here. In the last 6 years at the time of writing this article I have trained protection training with Marko Koskensalo. 2016, Radek Kupka (RADDOG) many times and in preparation for the worlds, Vasek Borek before the USA Nationals, Teemu Parvianen, Kelly Readman, Aaron Almeida our local decoy on Vancouver Island helped prep us for Jack's IPO 1 and 2 and a select few I've trusted in seminars; Dominic Scarberry, Tommi Vanhala, Tim Cutter and Michael Lorraine. All some of the finest helpers. My training partners and people who have helped us to reach success in some way along the way(club) have been great people like Sandra and Henry Rushing, Lisa Tamblyn, Susan Mullins, Lasha Anguish, Rob Vylchenko, Radek Kupka, Federico Dela T Labistada, Michelle Rill, Frank Phillips, I seriously hope I'm not forgetting someone.

12. If you have the same dog again, what will you so different?

Nothing.

13. Is he / she social with people?

Jack is social but serious if you act stupid or enter his space without me there.

14. Any funny stories you want to share?

He earned the name Jack Tyson after biting Vice World Champion Aro's ear ⅓ off, not so sure that was funny at the time but afterwards telling the story of Aro's ear loss was.

15. If you can change 1 thing about the dog, what would it be?

Early onset food drive.

16. How was the dog like when he/ she as a puppy?

Jack was still calm and serious as a puppy, he showed active clear prey and frustration and would not hesitate to nip in frustration or show teeth if he didn't like you.

17. How was he / she like as he / she matured?

Later in life Jack has developed into a social stable dog with serious active aggression when needed. He is a pleasure to be around due to his calm friendly nature.

18. How are the dog's litter mates?

I believe they are all in Europe so I don't know much about them. Conan vom Clan Der Wolfe has placed podium placements 2 years in a row at the FMBB.

19. Is he / she social with other dogs?

He is dog neutral and if they are social he can be too.

20. Does the dog live in a house or a kennel?

He is laying at my feet in the evenings and spends the days in the kennel but also occasionally loose with me in the office.

Oma's Pride
2019 AWMA Nationals

Dog 62 - Wolfstans Justice (54702 NVBK BR)

Owner: James Wozencroft

Tactical jungle tracker dog.

Justice is now based out in Africa with his section living in the jungle where his main role is to protect endangered rhinos. His becoming one of Africa's most famous and successful canines as well as being one of the most feared.

Justice was trained at Wolfstan Kennels LTD, An international Canine training centre based in the UK. Their main role is procurement and training canines for military and police deployment. His training program was written and delivered by their training team.

Justice is a Belgian Malinois, a very good representation of the FCI purebred Belgian Malinois.

He is clear headed with a stable character but still with a high consistent drive and an attitude that allows him to have the correct approach to his training So he can reach the high levels needed for this role.

All canines from the UK national training centre are purposely selected for their role and go through various processes before they begin their specialist training.

Selection and procurement of any canine is done by Wolfstan's head trainer James Wozencroft.

Justice comes from a very consistent proven line of Belgian shepherds where they have been proven in both working and sport at a high level, having competed and represented their country and have many popular names in their pedigree.

This gave us a consistent litter, with the majority of brothers and sisters sharing many of the same qualities and characteristics.

Justice has a large strong bone structure, with good portions and composition to his body not only gives him looks but the correct movement, giving a massive advantage when these dogs get put through their paces.

They can do in excess over 20 miles in a day on live operations and do regular operational tracks of over 23km into live fire. This makes the physical ability of the dog just as important as it's mental.

Out in the jungle environment it's massively different to working in other environments that are more urban which meant we had to develop a different approach to working a dog in this harsh environment and condition where the jungle is dense with heat regularly reaches into and above 40 degrees, along with a vast amount of harsh terrain. Not to mention the dangers and hazards of working in a place like this from other animals and humans.

For a Dog to go fully operational and ready for any eventuality it takes around 3 years for that dog to reach its full potential, and that's with a high level of training most days.

Justice along with his handler and team have had many achievements and are still in live operation today.

At the time of this publication none of his achievements can be discussed or published due to legislation and court hearings.

Thanks to his trainers, handler and all his operational section staff he has become one of the best and strongest anti poaching dogs.

Dog 63 - Lorockmor Ragnar (BRN36150)

Owner: Laurie Stanley

1. How is he / she at home, out of work?

At home and out of work Ragnar is a great dog to be around and is extremely easy to live with. We have a large family so there are constantly people in and out the house. Ragnar is often around the elderly as well as young children and always acts appropriately when around them. He is very clear and level-headed at the age of 16 months. However, if a new person is around then he will make his presence known.

2. Describe his or her character with 5 words..

Strong, focused, confident, resilient and clear.

3. What is his / her best quality?

His overall nature. His willingness and drive to work yet calmness when placed in public environments e.g. on the train, in the pub, etc.

4. What is his / her least desirable attribute?

His least desirable attribute is that I have never known a dog to s**t as much as him.

5. Is he / she one of your favourite dogs of all time?

Yes, I would say he is my favourite, apart from my Labrador Pele.

6. What is his / her favourite activity?

When training in the KNPV system the bite work is most definitely his favourite. However, he really enjoys searching and swimming as well.

7. What is his / her biggest achievements?

None to date. Looking to title and gain his PH1.

8. Was he / she difficult to train?

Not particularly no. There is always going to be exercises that are more difficult than others but on a whole he takes to new tasks very quickly.

9. What's your favourite offspring of his / her?

He has none to date.

10. How heavy was or is he / she?

He is currently 38kgs.

11. Where is your training club and decoys who helped him / her?

My club is Lorockmor. Decoys and helpers are Ian Morgan, Sam Frost, Muz, Andrea, Asa Wright and Paul Harding.

12. If you have the same dog again, what will you so different?

Nothing. I am really happy with the journey so far so I would not have done anything different if I had the time again.

13. Is he / she social with people?

He is very social so I take him everywhere with me; to work, on the train, through city centres, to the pub. However, he can be sharp if approached the wrong way.

14. Any funny stories you want to share?

When he was a few months old I was getting the train back home from London. It was a two-and-a-half-hour train journey so I was on the platform waiting in plenty of time to make sure he went to the toilet. The time had passed and he had not gone before the train eventually arrived. We got on the train and started walking through the carriages looking for a seat, low and behold Ragnar then decided it was time to go to the toilet in front of everyone.

15. If you can change 1 thing about the dog, what would it be?

That he did not go to the toilet so much!

16. How was the dog like when he/ she as a puppy?

Ragnar was very confident and outgoing. From a pup he was on the train and coming to work with me every day. He was always a flyer from his very first training session.

17. How was he / she like as he / she matured?

He has matured into a big handsome dog. He is extremely powerful and knows how to use his weight well, but is also exceptionally light on his feet. He is very agile for his size as he jumps and flies through the air like a stag. Temperament wise he has matured into my ideal dog, high drive and still growing but very level-headed when needed.

18. How are the dog's litter mates?

There were only two in the litter. His sister was a great looking dog as well and was remarkably similar to him. She was the size of most males and is now a licenced police dog.

19. Is he / she social with other dogs?

Yes, he is very social with other dogs if they don't start anything. He is very boisterous when off the lead with others but loves to play even though it's quite physical. On lead he will walk and not bat an eyelid at other dogs even if they are going ballistic, he will just walk on past (one of my favourite things about him). But at the same time he won't tolerate a dog coming into his space and kicking off.

20. Does the dog live in a house or a kennel?

He lives in a kennel outdoors, however he does come in the house at times and is very well behaved.

Dog 64 - Dino te Lindert (BRN23586)

Owner: J Te Lindert

Born in Doetinchem Netherlands in the kennels of John te Lindert.

Was in the top three of the litter, and the wife of John picked him out to keep and train.

Dino has very extreme drives. The trick of it all is how will these drives develop through time. Dino has a high will to please. More often in this bloodline the character may not be easy to reach. The extreme drives can block the thinking process of these dogs. But with Dino it came out perfect. He was able to channel the extreme passion for biting, apport, search yet you could reach him and mold him into a competition dog for the knpv. He is extremely social and a very honest dog. This bloodline is known to be able to shift well between family and work environment. He has sons certified as dual purpose police canines worldwide. His semen is shipped worldwide.

When you work him and train him for competition he can become very smart in the routine. It is important to train him in different environments so he can not anticipate what the routine is. A very intelligent dog and has the ability to work on mental pressure. He will not back down, nor will his bite deteriorate if he is challenged through training pressure and perfection in his work.

The department of defense in the USA has used him as stud. They asked to have his genetic testing done in the Finland laboratory mydogdna. He was cleared of all genetic tests and approved for the American DoD program together with his x rays. He has proven himself as a stud. Offspring are work quality pups, most likely to have his beautiful red color.

JMPolicedogs.com Netherlands where he enjoys retirement

Dog 65 - Extremus Indi (BRN21038)

Owner: Darren Priddle

Now 8.5 years old, Indi is a proven and highly successful producer to many working and operational dogs within both the UK and Internationally.

At Extremus, we base the foundation of our breeding programme on the production of consistent, balanced and multidisciplinary working litters. Indi is the cornerstone of this programme. She may not have the strongest bite or the most drive or even have the most heart. What Indi does have is the ability to perform consistently well at any task she is put to. Some dogs excel in one or two areas, Indi surpasses expectation with every objective. Something she has passed onto the 5 litters we have raised with her.

Granted, some of the puppies she has produced with 4 different sires have not made the standard at which we set, but consistently she has gone on to produce above a 75% success rate in dual purpose working dogs. I do not mean that she has produced dogs that have the potential, I mean she has produced dogs that have either licensed, been certificated, titled or have street experience and capability. Proven and documented.

I am a big believer that the Dam is more important when producing a working litter than the Sire, although I will always choose a Sire that compliments or adds to the female in question.

Police, Security, Military, Anti-Poaching, Sport; she has produced dogs that have been highly successful in all of these disciplines. When I first purchased her many people told me she was not worth my effort as her bloodline was poor, there was nerve in her line, she would not produce well. Whilst I took on board their opinion, I decided to judge the dog in front of me; she repaid my trust and confidence in her tenfold.

Any decent breeder worth their salt that produces operational working dogs with care and passion, should be striving for the level of success that she has consistently produced. Many would have written her off; does not hit hard enough, does not have a push grip, is not calm enough on the bite. Whilst others strive for a perfection they will never achieve, I look for a dog that ticks as many boxes as possible and can do pretty much anything you ask, anytime, anywhere to a minimum of a good standard. That is the type of dog I choose for my breeding programmes. Indi is and has always been that type of dog.

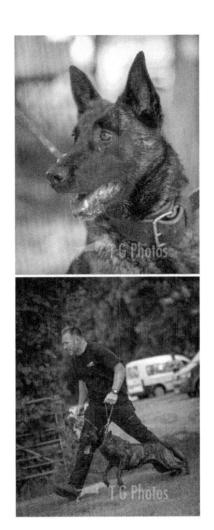

Dog 66 - Lorockor Simba (BRN32775)

Owner: Viki Frater

1. How is he / she at home, out of work?

I can only make a description of Simba outside of work based on the now as he is ever changing. It has taken me 3 years to get him as balanced as I would like him. As a pup and adolescent dog he was always in work mode and I couldn't really take him anywhere.

He is now 3 and outside of work he is mostly a calm (for a malinois) happy and confident dog. He doesn't really do anything wrong, he's not naughty or disobedient and he can entertain himself whilst remaining close and respectful of what I expect from him. I can take him anywhere new with me and he will just lay down and chill if we are alone: He wont switch off if someone is there, the best I can get is a down stay with a lot of staring and growling, but hey I love that about him.

I can walk him with a pack of dogs in spacious public places and he minds his own business. He isn't reactive to anything that isn't threatening or a drive trigger and will only hunt now if I allow him to. I had a few unexpected obstacles along the way; controlling his drive to hunt and kill which kicked in after a sheep related incident. But in general he is a pleasure to now have out on walks and hikes as long as I always stay one step ahead of him and don't get complacent.

I get a lot of people quite pleasantly shocked at his obedience and behaviour on pack walks knowing his character and what he is capable of. He has a very short fuse on his aggressive side so I have to be careful with situations that cause over arousal with people as it can quickly switch to something aggressive.

Simba will not allow anyone (including myself) to bully him or man handle him. I've always had to play fair game with him in a very calm way that still applies the necessary mental pressure, and in return he is well behaved and affectionate; he is very clear about what he likes and what he doesn't like; but is still susceptible to growth and small steps of submission. He's not a sociable dog, keeps to his own outside and observes from a distance. The odd occasion I've had him in the house with someone he has muzzle attacked them. This is something I love and wouldn't change.

2. Describe his or her character with 5 words..

Confident, focused, sharp, intense and affectionate.

3. What is his / her best quality?

His best quality I would say is his deep rooted man aggression. He has high levels of sharp intent in his work. It's not a game for him. Very serious in his work.

4. What is his / her least desirable attribute?

His least desirable attribute is definitely that relentless bark. Mali's have a habit of overkill with barking. It starts off ok with a nice kick off to alert/deter/warn whatever the job may be, then when all of the other dogs have shut down he's still barking. There's no gain from it. I think he just gets into such a state of arousal that he can't help it. I've probably told him to shut the fuck up more times than I can count.

5. Is he / she one of your favourite dogs of all time?

Simba is undoubtedly my second favourite dog of all time. Everyone who knows me knows of the dobermann with 1st place, however Simba is very close behind for completely different reasons. He is by far the best dog I have owned and I have a great respect and admiration for him. He is everything I ever wanted in a dog and more.

6. What is his / her favourite activity?

Favourite activity would be bite work of course. He was born for it. His whole body shakes with adrenaline just thinking about it. It's a pleasure to watch him work knowing how much he loves it.

7. What is his / her biggest achievements?

I'd say his biggest achievement was his insane progression up the working dog ladder in just 6 months. I took him training for the first time at 18 months old after doing nothing since he was 4 months old and within 6 months he was performing at a top level. He achieved more in that 6 months than I could have ever hoped for and built up a reputation as a solid top dog.

8. Was he / she difficult to train?

Simba was not difficult to train however that is more to do with my habitual methods rather than his personality. I had the fortunate opportunity to work alongside a phenomenal dog trainer for 3 years rehabilitating severely aggressive dog's. Thankfully because of this, my ability to train and control a dog like Simba is second nature and doesn't really require a lot of effort from me. All of the training is done in normal day to day activities such as walking, hiking and general living. I see many people struggle using double the effort with dogs that have much less about them. Without my past training and experience I would have likely struggled or ruined the dog. But thankfully I was fully prepared!

9. What's your favourite offspring of his / her?

Simba does not have any offspring, YET! I'd love to see what would come from a mating with the right bitch.

10. How heavy was or is he / she?

He currently weighs about 33 kilo ish, I never really weigh him.

11. Where is your training club and decoys who helped him / her?

The two lads who did an amazing job with his foundation work are from Sunderland; Dalton Rush and Michael Hutchinson. I then spent 4 days a week at Lorockmor for about 8 months and have trained multiple times with Bullvision. I now train at numerous clubs all over the UK depending which one is closer but my top two remain Lorockmor and Bullvision. Lorockmor have fantastic facilities and Scott Bullvision is an outstanding decoy. I always gain the most from training at these places.

12. If you have the same dog again, what will you so different?

If I could start again what would I do differently. Well in general there isn't anything I really dislike about Simba that could be changed by doing things differently. If I had to choose something I'd say maybe more bite work without conflict. Really work on the endurance and bite mechanics without all the crash bang wallop. But then again that could take away from his ability to thrive under conflict if it all became a non threatening situation. There are things I would like to have done but it would cost me something I love about him. So I guess I'd do everything the same. I always think about this stuff and always land on the same outcome: he is everything I want in a dog.

13. Is he / she social with people?

Simba is not sociable with people. As a pup he couldn't be let off lead around people as he would just bite everyone he never switched off from work mode. I've been slowly balancing him out and at 3 year old , in certain situations, I can put him into a neutral state in outdoor public places as long as whoever is with me follows very specific instructions. Indoors, at home, any other place is a no go.

14. Any funny stories you want to share?

He muzzle punched the vet in the face once when she checked on him after his sedative injection, that was pretty funny. I did tell her that he would need two to knock him out.

15. If you can change 1 thing about the dog, what would it be?

If I could change one thing it would 100% be his bark. I'd give him one much deeper, like that of my dobermann. Something more intimidating.

16. How was the dog like when he/ she as a puppy?

The only way to describe Simba as a puppy is to compare him to a tv character. Watch Ace Ventura Pet detective and look out for the crazy ass tribe fighter who is brought into the fight ring in a bag. He was absolutely ridiculous, if he had been an adult dog he would have been a danger to myself and society. So much so that I doubted whether I could balance him and almost sold him. It's funny and cute when they are that small but it's no joke to have those characteristics in an adult dog.

17. How was he / she like as he / she matured?

Simba has matured into a wonderful young dog. He is really starting to find a nice work/life balance in his own mind without it affecting his performance. I don't have to put a lot of pressure on him now. He's happy and he knows what I expect from him. If I'm cool he's cool. It's a nice bond.

18. How are the dog's litter mates?

I'm not sure what his litter mates are up to, I have seen his brother who is a very civil real type dog.... that's about it. The repeat matings did not meet the same standard.

19. Is he / she social with other dogs?

Simba is fantastic with other dogs. It's one of my top priorities and the thing I invest the most time into training. Mostly because my doberman is an asshole who won't tolerate ill mannered dogs.

20. Does the dog live in a house or a kennel?

Simba lives wherever I live. Indoors, outdoors, van life and home life. He's always with me.

Dog 67 – Yuko (AM02735107)

Owner: Stefan Leca

Where do I start?! Yuko was 8 weeks old when I got him from a breeder in Cambridge now, he is 9 years old and 2 months where did all that time go! Now he is retired, and he is enjoying the family life you don't even know he is there, but when he was operational he was in my van from day one, coming with me everywhere to work or social.

He always had a strong character which I had to shape, for him to fit my lifestyle including my family.

I guess to describe his character best words are smart, civil, social, dominant, boldness.

His best quality was that civil aggression when the teeth and saliva were coming out and whoever was in front of us always had to take a step back.

His less desirable attribute is his size only 31 kg

Yes 100% he is the best dog I ever owned/worked for security work.

His favourite activity is playing with the ball, his drive for the ball was always high and that's why it was easy in a way to train him.

This are his achievements:

- NASDU level 2 certificate

- NASDU track and search certificate 2011
- NASDU 1st place in Patrol and Handler Protection 2012 Trials
- NASDU 2nd place in competition 2012 Trials
- NASDU Best bite work 2012 Trials
- NASDU 1ST place in 2013 Winner of security working dog Trials
- DOG AND HANDLER AWARD 2013 awarded by The Worshipful Company of Security Professional
- NASDU 1ST place in 2014 Winner of security working dog Trials
- DOG AND HANDLER AWARD 2014 awarded by The Worshipful Company of Security Professional
- NASDU 1ST place in 2015 Winner of security working dog Trials
- DOG AND HANDLER AWARD 2015 awarded by The Worshipful Company of Security Professional
- 2015 1st place UKPPDA Trials
- 2015 1ST place BIPDT Trials
- Qualified BH, IPO1, IPO2
- 2015 BPSCA Handler Protection winner
- 2014 BPSCA Obedience winner

Favourite offspring is a male from him that I once met on a trial but do not remember the dog's name or the handler.

All the training was done by me and a friend of mine that is not known to the industry up until 2 years old but then I needed him to open up and to show me that real aggression and Danny Lines was the man, I went to his club one day and then I started training with him every day.

I have made so many mistakes with him due to my lack of knowledge at the time, I wouldn't go in too many details but yes definitely would change some things specially tracking and searching for property.

Yes, very social but he has a really good switch you can play with him now and in the next second if I give him the command, he will bite no hard fillings. Me and Danny Lines worked hard on this.

We had our funny moments but will not share them as this book won't be big enough.

If I could change one thing it would be his size.

As a puppy he was full of drive, typical Malinois attached to your leg, so it was hard work.

After the training was completed, he relaxed, and he understood the work very well and the home environment.

He is dominant with other dogs but not aggressive. He always knew when to approach a dog and how to do it.

He was in the kennel up until a year ago but now is in the house.

Dog 68 – Rico (BRN28915)

Owner: David DeSimone

1. How is he / she at home, out of work?

At home, and out of drive he shuts off well. He lives in the kennel, or crate when not working.

2. Describe his or her character with 5 words..

Tenacious, pronounced, resilient, biddable, intelligent

3. What is his / her best quality?

His best quality is his resilience. He works through negative stimuli, and his ability to work in chaotic, or stressful environments.

4. What is his / her least desirable attribute?

His aloofness. He's as civil a dog as you will find. There is absolutely no margin of error when out in public.

5. Is he / she one of your favourite dogs of all time?

He's the only male I've ever kept in 27 years of training, breeding, and procuring dogs. I've been fortunate with strong dogs, but until Rico, I've never seen a stud that I've wanted to feed, and take care of from the whelping box to the grave. He's my favorite out of all the dogs I've actually seen. Django Sommers is my favorite based on what I read.

6. What is his / her favourite activity?

Other than bite work, his favorite activity is diving under water for his ball. Each year he has gone deeper, and stays underwater longer. Watching him problem solve in that environment is as rewarding as personal protection.

7. What is his / her biggest achievements?

I would say competing in Iron Will, and Fright Night before he was two were his biggest accomplishments. Without a regimented obedience schedule Rico won't win a competition anytime soon, however it's an excellent test to evaluate the character of a dog. Not to mention it's fun.

8. Was he / she difficult to train?

No he's very biddable. He will work for food, praise, or a prey item. With that being said I wouldn't want him being my first dog as a green handler. He will not tolerate an unfair correction.

9. What's your favourite offspring of his / her?

As of right now Kona (28269) Rico (28915) is my favorite offspring, because they are producing, and we now have the ability to see, and evaluate their offspring.

I will say I'm liking all the combinations so far. I believe Rico has close to forty offspring, and I know of one pup that didn't work. If that trend continues I can't ask for anything more.

10. How heavy was or is he / she?

He's 80lbs.

11. Where is your training club and decoys who helped him / her?

I train in Anderson S.C. with Charlie Randolph.

Decoys that have worked Rico.

Charlie Randolph

Barry Walton

Malinois Sam

Mike Wentworth

Cody Girten

Tai Nero

Josh Bailey

Andre Carmichael

John Revere

Garland Whorley

Robert Garland

Justin Rigney

Eric Stridon

Marcus Alexander

Dez Lynch

Rodney Tank Mosley

Delroy Lewis

Calvin Wilbon

Andrew Coffelt

Josh Magee

Nic Tolson

Malik Whitfield

A few more but I can't remember everyone's name.

12. If you have the same dog again, what will you so different?

The only thing I would do differently is teach leg bites first. It's easier to transition to arm bites, if the dog was started on legs.

13. Is he / she social with people?

No, he was social as a pup up until 5-6 months.

14. Any funny stories you want to share?

Well I have plenty. One time Charlie was working him, and the fight was going on 5-6 minutes. Charlie took him to the ground, and put his entire weight on him. A few seconds later in the video you see both dog, and decoy rise up, and Rico flip Charlie off his back. Funny, and impressive all at the same time.

15. If you can change 1 thing about the dog, what would it be?

He doesn't like to be handled, he tolerates it to a degree with me, but even that has limitations. He's tactile sensitive, not too misconstrued with pain sensitivity.

16. How was the dog like when he/ she as a puppy?

He's not changed. What I saw as a pup, is exactly what he matured into as an adult.

17. How was he / she like as he / she matured?

He continues to get stronger. There were times early on, when the second time we worked on a scenario, you would see a notable improvement. He wants to dominate in the fight, and when he's put into uncomfortable positions he has a tendency to put his power into his body. Charlie was relentless in conveying to him that all that power needs to be in the bite to make the pressure go away. Perhaps it was immaturity, or lack of experiences to draw off of. To a degree I'm speculating, but that's my best guess.

18. How are the dog's litter mates?

Out of 40 pups I've had negative feedback on one. Out of the ones I've seen I'm pleased so far with the combinations, and offspring.

19. Is he / she social with other dogs?

Yes although to the untrained eye he may not appear to be because he's so reactive.

20. Does the dog live in a house or a kennel?

He lives in the kennel, and at night he comes into the crate. I was fortunate early on to learn the importance of those tools. Meeting and seeing Bernhard Flinks dogs years ago made an impression. When I pull a dog out to work, I know that if it's not giving me a 100%, it's not because it's drive has been satisfied all day chasing squirrels, and smelling flowers. Usually with a herder that's not an issue, however if I manage the small things, usually the big things don't seem to be an issue.

Dog 69 – Repo (BRN27530)

Owner: Jay Raw

1. How is he / she at home, out of work?

As of today he's an old man. Out of drive he's a somewhat stubborn happy old guy. He's kind of a one owner type dog, not mean but always pushy.

2. Describe his or her character with 5 words..

Flammable, courageous, forward, stubborn, pushy

3. What is his / her best quality?

He has a few nice qualities but if I could only mention 1 it would be that he's always ready for conflict. Flammability

4. What is his / her least desirable attribute?

His grips!

5. Is he / she one of your favourite dogs of all time?

Yeah he makes my top 10 best dogs I've owned.

6. What is his / her favourite activity?

Biting or killing things.

7. What is his / her biggest achievements?

That's classified information.

8. Was he / she difficult to train?

Very difficult to train. He was a very flammable dog, several trainers thought he should be euthanized. I saw no problem with him but I will say he was a very difficult dog to train.

9. What's your favourite offspring of his / her?

I'd like to reserve this as he's not done producing. He's got a few notable sons out there.

10. How heavy was or is he / she?

61-68 lbs depending what he's eating or activity level, stays around 65 lbs.

11. Where is your training club and decoys who helped him / her?

No specific training club, worked with a few groups in Holland but not one club. He was a nomadic dog and still is.

12. If you have the same dog again, what will you so different?

More grip development and take my time to just let him be a pup.

13. Is he / she social with people?

By temperament he's social meaning he's not defensive or suspicious, but he's very happy to bite and since I've raised him a certain way he sometimes looks at people as prey items. In his defense he's social about wanting to bite you.

14. Any funny stories you want to share?

One time the dog sat in fire.

There was a barrel of garbage burning outside in the yard. I was working his position and his placements. I told the dog to back up, he thought I said place, he decided that his placement should be inside the barrel while trash was burning, so what does he do, he jumps in the burning barrel. I panicked trying to tell him his release command, because of the panic in my voice and the way I was frantically saying it he didn't recognize that I was releasing him. Anyway after about 20 second it felt like I said his recall, he jumps out of the barrel and comes to a recall position, limps into a heel and walks alongside me. I checked his underside. Balls, tail and ass burnt, all because he thought I said place. I'm sure it was less than 20 secs but it felt like 20 secs.

15. If you can change 1 thing about the dog, what would it be?

GRIPS

16. How was the dog like when he/ she as a puppy?

Flammable, high drive, unclear and selfish. Very difficult dog to raise.

17. How was he / she like as he / she matured?

Calmer but still flammable. About half as nasty but more refined with a Dr Jekyll Mr Hyde attitude at times. Way more manageable. He changed around the middle of 2 years, almost 3 years old.

18. How are the dog's litter mates?

Only 3 were good in my opinion out of 8 I believe. I know the Belize Consulate tried to buy his sibling for 27,000 I believe. The rest I believe were flat or average.

19. Is he / she social with other dogs?

He's dog dominant and low roller ace for conflict. Has some inner species rank for sure, always pushy.

20. Does the dog live in a house or a kennel?

These days he goes back and forth but more so in the house. He's earned it so he's retired to the house now.

Dog 70 – Rocky

Owner: Jerry Bradshaw

Rocky came to me in a group of police dogs from a vendor in Holland. I had just retired my SchH competition dog Arrow SchH 3 because of a stroke, and I liked some things about how Rocky worked, including his blazing fast entries and his big powerful grip. But he was not anything like Arrow. He was Bigger and physically stronger, and not quite as high strung. He of course was totally green at only 11 months old, and I was used to working a highly precise well trained SchH dog that went to USA Nationals in 1996. Going from a national quality trained SchH3 to handling a green dog again was difficult for me. I told people Arrow was like a well-worn baseball glove. He and I knew everything about each other, he fit me, I knew his strengths and weaknesses and he knew mine. Rocky was all new. Sharp edges, and all. He didn't have the experience or the training, and at first I didn't like him. Mainly because he wasn't Arrow.

Rocky became a great trained dog once I realized he never would be Arrow, and I needed to look at him not in comparison but as an individual. We trained hard, and got our BH at 3. I don't show my young dogs until I feel they are solidly mature, mentally and physically. He showed out beautifully. We then embarked on our PSA career. We finished it at PSA 3 but sadly at a little over 7 years old he developed a cancer in the jaw and shortly thereafter he had to be put down. In training I called him the "choir boy" because he learned new things so easily and always for the most part did them right, right away. He contrasted with his contemporary Ricardo, my other PSA dog in every aspect of temperament.

He taught me a lot over our career together. We travelled all over the country chasing PSA titles. Back then it cost may be $100 to fly a dog one way to the west coast, and we went everywhere. Los Angeles, Sacramento, Las Vegas. We showed more than we should have but we were also promoting the sport of PSA in new areas of the country. He sailed through his beginning titles in PSA. We struggled a lot with the call off in PSA 2 which at the time was a static picture of the decoy doing jumping jacks, and he knew the picture! So many times we were only that exercise away from passing PSA 2. We failed a lot at PSA 2! Eventually we sorted that out, and where he really shined was at the PSA 3 level. Surprise scenarios were his territory. He was clear and fast and powerful in bite work, and controllable in obedience. Rocky lived at a time in PSA where LaMont Houston's dog Porter was beginning his reign as one of the greatest PSA dogs of all time. I lost Rocky in June preceding the 2003 PSA 3 National Championship in November. Rocky was the odds on Favorite to win nationals that year, and beat Porter, had he not gotten sick. In the end, Ricardo won that championship in 2003. I always say he did it for his brother.

1. How is he / she at home, out of work?

Rocky was a civil dog so if he didn't know you he didn't like you. New kennel techs were always surprised at how once he warmed up to you he was a lover.

2. Describe his or her character with 5 words..

He was somewhat soft, strong, civil, fast, bit hard.

3. What is his / her best quality?

His entries on the suit in the bicep were astonishingly fast and he was about 78 lbs so he came in powerfully.

4. What is his / her least desirable attribute?

His softness to the handler.

5. Is he / she one of your favourite dogs of all time?

Yes, he was a pleasure to train, if you did it right (often I made mistakes) and he had nerves of steel.

6. What is his / her favourite activity?

Bitework.

7. What is his / her biggest achievements?

PSA 3.

8. Was he / she difficult to train?

The softness made him anticipate sometimes, that was the biggest challenge.

9. What's your favourite offspring of his / her?

I never bred him.

10. How heavy was or is he / she?

75-80 lbs.

11. Where is your training club and decoys who helped him / her?

Tarheel Canine PSA in Sanford NC and Capital Cities K9 in Baltimore MD.

12. If you have the same dog again, what will you so different?

He caused me to change a lot of techniques to accommodate his handler softness. Especially using less force on the call-off to initially teach the behavior more motivationally.

13. Is he / she social with people?

He was neutral outside the kennel. Didn't really like strangers, but people in his circle saw the real sweet social side of him.

14. Any funny stories you want to share?

We were showing for the level 3 in West Palm Beach, Florida. The scenario was that the dog was in a baby pool behind me. It was made to look like the PSA 2 call off but instead the decoys (multiple) charged at you and it was a call-off of the charging decoys. The decoys started at me, I called him to heel to send him down field and he took my legs out from me and all I remembered was looking at the sky and hearing the impact of the hit on one of the decoys. Kind of knocked the wind out of me a little!

15. If you can change 1 thing about the dog, what would it be?

Be a little more handler hard, not much, just a little.

16. How was the dog like when he/ she as a puppy?

I got him at 10 months.

17. How was he / she like as he / she matured?

Confident, quiet, impressive, driven.

18. How are the dog's litter mates?

Don't know any of them.

19. Is he / she social with other dogs?

He liked females. I never let him around other males.

20. Does the dog live in a house or a kennel?

He lived in a kennel. He got lazy when he came inside the house!

Dog 71 – Ricardo (BRN515)

Owner: Jerry Bradshaw

I first saw Ricardo at KNPV Nationals in 1999 I believe. He was handled by Tino Kleine Schaars. When I saw his obedience (heads up heeling) which was unusual for a KNPV dog, I was impressed. Big dog seemed easily close to 90 lbs. He was fast and hit like a truck. At his club he routinely took decoys down. After leaving the KNPV Nationals that year, I was on a buy trip for dogs elsewhere in Holland, and I got a call from a vendor who said, "remember that big dog with the floppy ears from nationals? He is for sale!" At the time I wasn't looking for another personal dog but Joe Morris the co-founder of PSA was looking, and so we went to see Tino and Ricardo. They showed us the stick attack, and up close it was even more impressive. When they asked Joe if he was interested in the dog, he said to my surprise "no, I don't like the ears and if I breed him, I don't want pups with soft ears." They looked at me and I said "this dog needs to come back to America." So I agreed to buy him.

In Holland after he got his X-Rays done, Tino dropped him at the vendor's place, and left. He was coming out of his anesthesia still when we had to load up to head to Schipol Airport at about 3:30 am. The vendor said go get Ricardo and load him up. So I went to his kennel where he was sleeping, and I made some noise to wake him, and as I grabbed the latch he looked at me with dead eyes (I had seen that look in a dog's eyes before) and I let him be. I told the vendor "hes gonna smoke me if I go in there, he's coming out of anesthesia, its dark and I really am not interested in getting bit right now." The vendor took my leash and walked off mumbling "American pussy!" when he opened the kennel door Ricardo sounded like a fucking lion and he barely got the door closed before Ricardo hit the door full on. The vendor walked back to me mumbling curse words in Dutch. "So are you a Dutch pussy?" I asked him. He called Tino to come from his house to move the dog 30 yards from the kennel to a crate in the van!

When I got the dog home, I took him out and walked him, and he was neutral, his eyes were cold, and we walked and I wondered what the actual fuck I did in buying this dog! Tino told stories of Ricardo and how he came to him, after putting multiple handlers in the hospital and at least one on permanent disability. I was young and stupid and in over my head. Ricardo lived for another 10 years after I got him at 4 years old, and we never got in a fight. I respected him, and adjusted my training, so as to not provoke a retaliation. He taught me a lot about how people can try and bully dogs in training until they run up on a Ricardo. He was every bit of 95 lbs, muscled like a stone. You didn't want him to bite you without equipment. He was the single most powerful dog I ever worked with to this day.

He earned PSA 3 at consecutive trials in early 2003 and won the PSA 3 National Championships later that year, as I said, for his "brother" Rocky. He trained many decoys for the sport. The first time Sean Siggins PSA Director of Decoys caught him in early 2001 I think Ricardo broke Sean's ribs on the frontal catch. I retired him in 2003, and he continued to train decoys and be a demo dog at seminars. He passed away peacefully at 14 years old at my home.

1. How is he / she at home, out of work?

Outside of work he was calm, settled easily, and a very steady dog.

2. Describe his or her character with 5 words..

Prey Monster, fast, strong, unyielding.

3. What is his / her best quality?

His flying into the grip.

4. What is his / her least desirable attribute?

His excessive prey fixation.

5. Is he / she one of your favourite dogs of all time?

Yes, he was one of my best teachers.

6. What is his / her favourite activity?

Biting.

7. What is his / her biggest achievements?

PSA 3 (back when you had to get 80% in OB and all protection scenarios to pass) and National Championship PSA 3 2003.

8. Was he / she difficult to train?

Retraining him to PSA from KNPV habits was the single most challenging training I have done to date on a personal dog. He is still the ONLY KNPV PH1 to be converted to PSA 3.

9. What's your favourite offspring of his / her?

Didn't know most of them.

10. How heavy was or is he / she?

95lbs.

11. Where is your training club and decoys who helped him / her?

Tarheel Canine PSA and Capital Cities K9

12. If you have the same dog again, what will you so different?

Not get him at 4!

13. Is he / she social with people?

Not real social. Extreme neutrality. Only cared about his handler, period, to interact with.

14. Any funny stories you want to share?

At a pre-PSA protection event (K9 Pro Sports famous trial in Brooksville FL) I just finished the bite work routine, where Ricardo failed the call-off (bit on call-off). The steward was Rik Wolterbeek, and he knew the dog from Holland and had a healthy respect for him. He handed me my leash and collar, as I reached for it, Ricardo saw the Judge who was a USPCA judge named Noel Coward, writing on his clipboard. Ricardo broke and went into a full sprint downfield toward him. I frantically tried to recall him, to no effect. The crown in the stands was substantial and you heard a collective gasp as Ricardo launched at Noel's bicep, who deflected him with the metal clipboard at the last second. As Ricardo went tumbling, Decoy Gus Artiles jumped in front of Noel, and took the bite. I hurried to him and put the leash and collar on before outing him, and quickly left the field completely embarrassed. At the awards banquet Noel approached me, and I was certain I was about to get a lecture (and rightly so) about controlling such a powerful animal. Instead he asked if I would sell him the dog! I politely declined.

15. If you can change 1 thing about the dog, what would it be?

His insane prey reflex.

16. How was the dog like when he/ she as a puppy?

Didn't know him then.

17. How was he / she like as he / she matured?

Only knew him as an adult.

18. How are the dog's litter mates?

He and a dutch shepherd female in Holland produced a ton of KNPV dogs. He only produced anything good with that one female to my knowledge.

19. Is he / she social with other dogs?

Never let him around other dogs except a few times to breed him. Otherwise neutral.

20. Does the dog live in a house or a kennel?

Most of his working life in a kennel, last few years as he aged he lived inside.

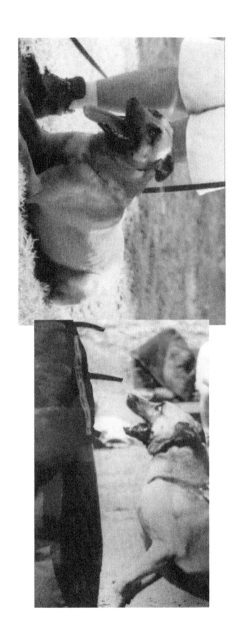

Dog 72 - Q'Azam (FCI RISH059/Q)

Owner: Felix Ho, Belgium

1. How is he / she at home, out of work?

Azam is calm and easy at home, very good with children, doesn't bark for nothing.

2. Describe his or her character with 5 words..

Friendly, willing, driven, devoted, intelligent.

3. What is his / her best quality?

His will for biting and the quality of his grip, both in the arms and in the legs.

4. What is his / her least desirable attribute?

He is not very talented in tracking.

5. Is he / she one of your favourite dogs of all time?

He is my favourite at the moment.

6. What is his / her favourite activity?

Biting.

7. What is his / her biggest achievements?

Making training a lot of fun.

8. Was he / she difficult to train?

Not at all.

9. What's your favourite offspring of his / her?

I haven't gotten to breed him yet as my current breeding female is his mother.

10. How heavy was or is he / she?

31 kg.

11. Where is your training club and decoys who helped him / her?

DTC Ghoy NVBK with my friend Christoph Joris.

12. If you have the same dog again, what will you so different?

I would be more patient.

13. Is he / she social with people?

He's very social. Anyone can pat him.

14. Any funny stories you want to share?

Everyday is fun with Azam.

15. If you can change 1 thing about the dog, what would it be?

More expression and thicker ears.

16. How was the dog like when he/ she as a puppy?

Super grip.

17. How was he / she like as he / she matured?

His good qualities magnify.

18. How are the dog's litter mates?

I also kept his brother Q'Ambush and trained him in IPO. We achieved his IGP2 at 2.5 years old. Ambush is a bit difficult for high points in IPO. He ended up serving in the elite Special Duty Unit in the Hong Kong Police. His new job description is "Anti-Terrorists Assault Dog". I also kept two half siblings from Azam born in 2020 (Dam: Chrissy). I'm very happy with them.

19. Is he / she social with other dogs?

He is social with other dogs and animals.

20. Does the dog live in a house or a kennel?

He lives in the kennel.

Dog 73 – Kasino (BRN24225)

Owner: Darrick Rose

I imported Kasino to the USA as a 8 week old pup from The Netherlands to be my next Personal Protection/ Competition K-9. Me and Kasino instantly became a perfect match for one another. I really enjoyed taking a pup and raising him to become one the BEST K-9s walking this earth. From the day I picked Kasino up at the airport we had major goals and we achieved them all. Kasino definitely had to be a strong minded dog to withstand the physical and mental beating that comes with the hard training that's required to become one of the GREATS in the Dog world. Together we've won several PSA trials, Iron Dog Competitions, and Personal Protection Competitions. I was offered $110,000.00 usd for Kasino and decided he's earned a right to live out his years with us, the family that loves him. Some dogs are just irreplaceable and we felt that Kasino was one of them. He's definitely a Top producer as well. Kasino is also known for having Super nerves, crushing fill grips, amazing drives, and second to none social Thank you for reading this short bio of my Bestfriend Kasino.

*Here's a few of Kasino Highlights
https://youtu.be/tGy4oKWXUK0

Dog 74 – Biko

Owner: Dean Galea

Biko is a great dog to live with at home and is calm and brilliant around my family. When at work he knows it's time to work. He is a brilliant all around dog.

In my opinion from owning Biko we have learnt that you can have a dog that can do both a dog that can be calm and loving in the home and around people but with one word turn into a full on protection dog. Bikos main thing I love about him is he has the heart of a lion and there is no giving up with him.

Least desired thing about him, he can be a pain in the backside when it comes to him being in a cage to transport he has to wear a muzzle due to Dan aging his teeth trying to demolish his cage. All saying that biko is my all time favourite dog we have done so much together in such a short time.

Biko's biggest achievement to date was coming 3rd in gold class, a sport dog in real I was over the moon with him that day and put a lot of dogs to shame.

Biko wasn't really hard to train. I purchased him with the help of my two bosses Naz Hussain and Danny Lines who went to Holland to get him tested and we brought him home. My favourite offspring of his is his son Nuko who is Biko crossed with a German Shepherd he has taken a lot of his dad's traits.

To date biko weights around the 40kg mark and his son nuko weighs around the 55kg

I mostly train my dogs at Britannia k9 training academy. But do train with a lot of other decoys also

Funny story about biko was him getting out of the back of my van on the a13 and not knowing about it until a lorry pulled me over and told me I had to walk 20mins down the motorway to find him sitting by the road looking like he was waiting for a cab. Few scratches on him but he was fine.

Biko is a social dog with all animals and people he lives in the house and in a kennel, a great all round dog couldn't ask for more.

Dog 75 – Deejay (BRN20833)

Owner: Bianca Jansma

1. How is he / she at home, out of work?

I bought deejay as a pup from 8 weeks old from a guy who was selling a bench for my other dog, and there at this guy's house was Deejay and he was for sale.

So I ended up buying the bench and puppy Deejay.

As a pup Deejay was a handful, very mischievous! No garbage bin was safe and barking a lot for attention when I was leaving him alone outside.

I taught him a lot at a young age, sit, heel, down and searching also bite work, we went to a lot of different places to get used to things.

2. Describe his or her character with 5 words..

Deejay is loyal, confident, kind to men / women / children and other dogs.

Natural leader, hard working, he loves every kind of sport, even when he is a bit older now.

A kid could do Sports with him!

3. What is his / her best quality?

His best quality is his leadership around other dogs, he understands dog language perfectly, and always ready to go to work, KNPV, IPO, agility or surveillance, he loves it all.

4. What is his / her least desirable attribute?

Least desirable trait.... Hmmm I can not name one, just because he got none, really nothing.

5. Is he / she one of your favourite dogs of all time?

Yes he is the best dog I ever owned, really a once in a lifetime dog, you can take him anywhere, always confident and clear headed in any situation.

6. What is his / her favourite activity?

His favorite activity is to go for a long walk and play fetch with his ball.

7. What is his / her biggest achievements?

His biggest achievement, there is more than one!

Certification PH1, IPO1, Night trials and was in a video clip Bizzey and Idaly, Laat Je Niet Gaan.

8. Was he / she difficult to train?

From day one, Deejay was an easy dog to train, very eager to learn new things and he was learning it faster than me!

9. What's your favourite offspring of his / her?

Deejay had one litter, and there are a few overseas and a few here in NL.

All Different kinds of sport and house dogs.

The character of the pups is mostly like their mother Baica, and not off Deejay.

10. How heavy was or is he / she?

Deejay is +- 42 kg and 27 inch high, and nice in proportion.

11. Where is your training club and decoys who helped him / her?

Deejay was going to 1 club for his IPO training, and later when he was switched to KNPV at PHV Enter, when are still in that club, Arjan Heuten was always the decoy at the club for Deejay. We trained regularly at different clubs, it's good for the dog, different helpers and surroundings.

12. If you have the same dog again, what will you so different?

If I would get this type of dog again, I would do everything exactly the same.

13. Is he / she social with people?

Deejay is very social with men/ women/ children. Also to other animals, if a dog is picking at him, he thinks bye bye, gives him or her the eye, turns around and walks away, but he will defend himself if necessary.

14. Any funny stories you want to share?

I have a Funny story about Deejay, once I bought salmon for Deejay, the fish was gone suddenly, and I was thinking look at him, he likes the salmon very much, but the truth was he buried the whole salmon under his blanket, and when I offered the salmon again, he literally make puke movements just like a human with his tongue out. Was so funny to see. He never eats fish.

15. If you can change 1 thing about the dog, what would it be?

There is not much to say to this question, I don't want to change anything about Deejay.

16. How was the dog like when he/ she as a puppy?

Deejay was as a puppy a very naughty, chewing on stuff he should not be chewing on, shoes, stealing laundry, chewing on the wooden bench, the garbage bin was never safe, always harassing my older dog Xeno.

All the flowers out of their flower pot, and he stands there, with the leaves in his mouth, looking at me "Huh? What did I do?" All kinds of things that pups do when they are young and mischievous.

17. How was he / she like as he / she matured?

Now that he is matured, he became a very stable clear headed dog. A great family dog and sport dog. At home he just wants to chill, and hang out with the kids. When he is at work, he will go go go.

19. Is he / she social with other dogs?

Deejay is very social with other dogs. On the leash or off, he does not bother other dogs, but when the other dog wants to play, he is like "Come on let's go and have fun".

20. Does the dog live in a house or a kennel?

Deejay lives most of his time inside the house, with the family, other dog and our 2 cats. But he will also be okay if I leave him outside in the kennel.

Dog 76 – Lex (BRN25192)

Owner: Chris Williams

1. How is he / she at home, out of work?

Fairly chilled out, but always alert and sharp.

2. Describe his or her character with 5 words..

Strong, dominant, athletic, loyal yet super affectionate to me.

3. What is his / her best quality?

Great switch off, so high drive and committed in bite work but switches off after.

Very loyal, I can have visitors round stroking him for hours, once they leave, they can't come back in without me saying so, something he's done naturally.

4. What is his / her least desirable attribute?

Has to have something in his mouth on a walk, stick or bottle. Something I should have nipped in the bud when he was younger.

5. Is he / she one of your favourite dogs of all time?

He is THE favourite dog I've ever had.

6. What is his / her favourite activity?

Bitework or just being with me.

7. What is his / her biggest achievements?

Working trials CDEX, ZWP 1 & 2, UK tracking dog level 1.

8. Was he / she difficult to train?

Very easy to train, willingness to please like no other and no handler aggression.

9. What's your favourite offspring of his / her?

Not been mated.

10. How heavy was or is he / she?

39kg.

11. Where is your training club and decoys who helped him / her?

Wirral K9 Academy, I've mainly decoyed him, but Tom Parker was one of the first decoys to work him properly.

12. If you have the same dog again, what will you so different?

My biggest wish is that I could get him at 15 weeks when he first came to the uk. Knowing what I know now and not getting him at 10 months being his 4th owner. I would do more competitions with him.

13. Is he / she social with people?

Social with people to an extent if I'm there. Great with kids.

14. Any funny stories you want to share?

He escaped not long after I got him, was in a kenne run at the time outside, woke up after a nightshift to find him playing with the neighbours kids in the garden. Luckily no one got hurt and I put a roof on the run that day.

15. If you can change 1 thing about the dog, what would it be?

Not tolerating other intact male dogs.

16. How was the dog like when he/ she as a puppy?

Had him from 10 months old, playful, cheeky, quite dominant but more in a pushy way, fine with all dogs.

17. How was he / she like as he / she matured?

Became less tolerant of other male dogs, a lot more serious when working.

18. How are the dog's litter mates?

Litter mate to Rage who Rodney Stoute trained.

19. Is he / she social with other dogs?

Dominant with other dogs, not good around most male dogs.

20. Does the dog live in a house or a kennel?

Lives in the house, very clean and switches off.

Dog 77 – Evil (BRN28542)

Owner: Kristina Senter Carlisle

1. How is he at home, out of work?

Evil is a happy, carefree dog when not working. He's not a needy or anxious dog and will relax independently at home whether loose or kenneled. He enjoys being near his family though and has a pleasant, confident resting character that is easy to be around. In his space, he is always a clean and quiet dog. Never hyper, and never a dog that attempts to escape confinement.

2. Describe his character with 5 words-

Intense, explosive, clear, strong, bold.

3. What is his best quality?

There are many excellent dogs with intense drives and strong nerves. Evil is easily among the nicest of them. He's powerful, possessive, confident and forward. What I personally have great appreciation for in addition to these qualities however is Evil's clarity and stability. He works primarily in prey, but is capable of being a very serious dog if pushed, remaining always forward and strong. Even when in aggression, he is still a clear-headed dog. Even when very frustrated or possessive, I have never worried about him redirecting onto me.

4. What is his least desirable attribute?

I'd say probably that he's larger than my personal ideal size. There are pros and cons to his size however, and the power he brings to the table is hard to argue with.

5. Is he one of your favorite dogs of all time?

Unquestionably. I have been lucky to own several very nice dogs in my lifetime, but Evil is absolutely amongst the nicest I've seen in person. He's a memorable dog to those who see him, and even more so to those who work him. I count myself as very lucky to own him.

6. What is his favorite activity?

Bitework of course is his number one love, nothing comes close to his desire to bite. I'm sure that will be the same as most strong working dogs however, so I'll mention that his love of biting is followed closely by his love of eating. He's the single highest food driven dog I've ever owned.

7. What is his biggest achievement?

What set Evil apart for me wasn't just his own strengths and impressive qualities, it was his ability to reproduce them. Despite being a young dog himself, his offspring with a variety of females are already showing great promise as strong police prospects.

8. Was he difficult to train?

I cannot take credit for the majority of Evil's foundation training - that must go to his previous owner, Khoshaba

Younan, and those he trained with. My experience with training Evil however is that his intense drive level and physical power make him a challenging dog to work. He's not an easily compliant or controlled dog, hard to corrections and quick in his decisions. The combination of these things means you must be particularly smart in planning training sessions. That said, his food drive, clarity and stamina enables a high repetition of success for most of our sessions.

9. What is your favorite offspring of his?

With puppies all over the world, I'd be hard pressed to single only one out.

10. How heavy is he?

Evil is around 95lbs and a very easy keeper. It's noteworthy that despite being a large dog, his speed and agility are very impressive. He could effortlessly out-jump and outrun many of the more average sized dogs I've owned.

11. Where is your training club and decoys who helped him?

Since purchasing him, my primary help in decoying his has been my husband, Cameron Carlisle and our club in Fincastle, Virginia, USA.

12. If you have the same dog again, what will you do differently?

Since I purchased Evil as an adult, my primary hope is simply to have the opportunity to raise another like him myself.

13. Is he social with people?

Yes, he's very social. He can be overbearing when meeting new people, so he's not a dog I allow to often interact freely, but he can be walked through crowds or taken into any environment with confidence. He is most polite with children actually, and a very trustworthy dog for our toddler to be around. If we are not present however, he will not tolerate strangers entering our yard or home.

14. Any funny stories you want to share?

Let me think on this.

15. If you can change 1 thing about the dog, what would it be?

Honestly I don't say often that a dog is everything I want them to be, but thus far, Evil has met or exceeded every one of my expectations. Others may prefer a more dominant dog, or one faster to become nasty in defense, but those are not my personal preference.

19. Is he social with other dogs?

Yes, he is great with other dogs. He plays very well with our female dogs and even our intact male small pet dog and though as a habit we never allow male working dogs to interact freely, Evil never offers to fence fight or challenge other males.

20. Does the dog live in the house or kennel?

A combination of loose in the house, crated or out in the fenced yard.

Dog 78 – Dorie

Owner: Andre Meding

1. How is he / she at home, out of work?

Dorie is always on fire and she is always looking for something to bite and chew. The only place where she comes to rest is her kennel. Apart from her kennel she is just relaxed while driving in the car. There she is nearly some kind of hypnotized and also can sit still in the footwell of the car.

2. Describe his or her character with 5 words..

Prey drive, prey drive, prey drive, prey drive and prey drive.

3. What is his / her best quality?

Dorie has got a high amount of prey drive combined with the fact that she likes to use her teeth. So whenever there is an opportunity she will bite or chew things no matter what it is.

4. What is his / her least desirable attribute?

Dorie's best quality is also her least desirable attitude. She just wants to bite things the whole day.

5. Is he / she one of your favourite dogs of all time?

Dorie is for sure an extraordinary good female, but I personally like dogs with a higher amount of defensive drive and a lower stimulus threshold to it.

If I could just own one dog I would be unhappy owning a dog like Dorie. But as a second or third dog for having some fun Dorie is a very very good dog.

6. What is his / her favourite activity?

Dorie likes to bite and chew things. But one of her favourite activities during our walks is carrying branches.

7. What is his / her biggest achievements?

Dorie is not worked in common dog sport. I took part at several fun events or events for security service dogs handlers. She entered events in Belgium, England, Germany and the Netherlands since she was very young. Even Dorie is not built up correctly therefore she was used to build up young decoys at our own training group of the AVD e.V. she was very successful within these events.

Dorie won multiple puppy classes, bronze classes, long send suits and long send sleeves of the AVD e.V.. I think there had been a couple of AVD e.V. events where I came home with three trophies of her. Funny fact is that I was mostly not the handler during the events therefore I am mostly too involved that I do not have the time to enter all of my dogs on my own.

Dorie was entered in the demanding gold class of the AVD e.V. once where she became 2nd. Besides these trophies

Dorie did ZWPI, ZWPII and the AD25KM of the AVD e.V. at a young age and she joined international wild boar hunts two times and gained certifications for working on wild boars.

8. Was he / she difficult to train?

Dorie has got a low stimulus threshold to prey drive. No one who wants to work efficiently within common dog sports would work a dog with these thresholds and amount of drive with pleasure.

To me personally there was nothing hard to train, because there is nothing really trained. Dorie is a very natural and raw dog. On the dogfield she was used to building up decoys nearly her whole life, because her high amount of prey drive mostly "forgives" the most mistakes of ongoing decoys.

9. What's your favourite offspring of his / her?

There are no offspring of her so far. But she fulfills all of our claims to a stud female, she is health tested and the rest time will tell.

10. How heavy was or is he / she?

She is a tiny dog and she weighs around 20kgs.

11. Where is your training club and decoys who helped him / her?

Dorie is not so much trained. She was used to educating decoys from an early age and she took part in many events, especially in Belgium and the Netherlands nearly unprepared. Instead of farsighted training I mostly did just fun with her. In the recent past I prepared her a bit more for our own AVD e.V. events.

12. If you have the same dog again, what will you so different?

For Dorie itself it was maybe a bit thoughtless to be used to build up decoys. Inexperienced decoys make a lot of mistakes and it just speaks for the dog itself that it is still able to perform on the level it performs at.
But I will over think twice before doing that to another dog again, people you put your work in like young/ inexperienced decoys mostly move on if they think they have got everything learnt from you they thought they needed to.

13. Is he / she social with people?

Dorie is very social with people. She was also handled during competitions multiple times by other people.

14. Any funny stories you want to share?

It's not that funny, but I reserved a female from the litter Wolf and Kuno nearly a year before the litter was born. I knew the mother Wolf was very good from our events as she also won the demanding gold class of the AVD e.V. and nearly all of her offspring from a previous litter also done with Kuno.

In the meanwhile a friend of mine I also know from our events owning a presa canario, Cleem Clintjes, from the Netherlands became more and more interested in these dogs. He was also training with the breeder Erwin Caelen at his club of De Vurige Herder (NVDV) in Belgium.

To him the litter was sold out. As I like Cleem a lot and I thought it would fit very well that he and Erwin work together in the same club I resigned my reservation to him even though I was sure I missed a very good dog with this decision.

After the litter was born I got a call from Erwin that to all reservations another female was born and I took my chance to get it even now it was just the last pick. Everyone was happy afterwards and even though the story is not funny I find it some kind of special within a dog world with a lot of envy and resentment.

15. If you can change 1 thing about the dog, what would it be?

I am happy with Dorie. Maybe she could be a bit taller.

16. How was the dog like when he/ she as a puppy?

Dorie was raised in the house. She was very workable from a young age. To me personally it's a big difference if you own one dog or you already own more dogs and you buy an additional dog.

So Hannibal for example, another dog I own was raised alone as a single dog and I can tell you a thousand stories. On the other hand Dorie was dog number four and I did not have the same time for her as I had for Hannibal.

Also the reason I bought Hannibal had been to buy a companion dog a pet, I did not know about working dogs or dog sports. Within Dorie I bought an additional dog for having fun on the dog field and also I wanted to buy a female for breeding.

So the whole approach was completely different. In the end she does her thing from day one. She was a bit unsure in the beginning, but I think at the age of around 6 months she was able to do most of the stuff good adult dogs are able to do.

17. How was he / she like as he / she matured?

Dorie is very independent, she has got no real focus on other dogs or me as the handler. She is mostly controlled by her drive and her passion to bite or chew things. She is a real crazy dog and she does her own thing. All handlers who own a dog out of these two litters out of Wolf and Kuno will confirm their craziness.

18. How are the dog's litter mates?

All of Dorie's litter mates are handled within sports or security service. There are a lot of very very good dogs like Thor of Olaf Hütter, Worf and many more mostly handled within NVDV by members of De Vurige Herder.

I like a female called Nash of Bart, a member of De Heidehond in Gierle/Belgium, I think it will be the dog with the biggest amount of defensive drive within both litters. And for sure I really like Dax of Ian Morgan, a dog which was owned by Peter Franck of De Heidehond in Gierle/Belgium.

I decoyed him a couple of times, and the dog was also offered to buy, but I did not have the capacities to take him therefore I was also a bit involved when Ian took the dog. I saw Dax last time during the gold class of 5K-9 Workingdogs AVD e.V.'s annual UK event in 2020 and it was an outstanding performance of the dog, I think everyone would be happy to own him.

19. Is he / she social with other dogs?

Dorie is not interested in other dogs. Even the dogs of her own pack she does not really care about. She is always on a mission to find something to bite and chew.

20. Does the dog live in a house or a kennel?

Dorie lived the first two years of her life inside the house, but after that she lives in a kennel. It is also the only place where she can slow down and rest.

© Elli Hock

Dog 79 - Axel Bang Bang Von der Lönshütte
(BRN37942 / AU0906749)

Owner: Sati Gill

1. How is he / she at home, out of work?

Axel at home whether he is in a kennel or next to me is a very calm and level headed dog, but when he is loose guarding my property nobody can get near the perimeter. Axel has a very good guarding instinct that makes him the perfect deterrent for strangers.

2. Describe his or her character with 5 words..

Axel is very loyal, loving and social when out of drive. Once it's time to work he is a very high driven dog and a workaholic.

3. What is his / her best quality?

I would say his best qualities in his work is the dog's speed, he has great speed in achieving the bite.

4. What is his / her least desirable attribute?

Axel likes to see what is going on around him, he doesn't miss a trick. He can be quite noisy at times, this is probably his least desirable attribute.

5. Is he / she one of your favourite dogs of all time?

Axel is my favourite dog of all time, I have achieved a lot with this dog here in the UK and in Europe.

6. What is his / her favourite activity?

By far his favourite activity is bite work, he lives for it.

7. What is his / her biggest achievements?

The dog has achieved quite a lot in the trialling scene whether it be here in the UK or Germany. Puppy class 1st, Bronze class 1st, Silver class 1st, Gold class 1st, Championship class 1st, Long send sleeve 1st, Long send suit 1st, he has achieved these all multiple times. If not first he always came within the top 3. He has also won Defend and Pursue at level 3, he came 1st place then after that he always came within the top 3.

8. Was he / she difficult to train?

Yes at a young age Axel was a handful to train, but with the right training and guidance over time he became a pleasure to train, channelling his drive in the correct ways with the correct work making him into the dog he is today.

9. What's your favourite offspring of his / her?

To date Axels offspring are still young, so we are still watching them and assessing them weekly at our club. What we are seeing so far and the feedback we are getting from the owners of Axel's offspring is very promising and tells me these pups are full of potential.

10. How heavy was or is he / she?

Axel is 31kg in weight, 25 inches to the shoulder.

11. Where is your training club and decoys who helped him / her?

I am the owner of 5k-9 working dogs AVD .e.V in Iver Slough. We have a fantastic facility here with lots of environmental stations to suit all dog training needs. I also have a number of great decoys around me to help progress dogs of all different ages to all different standards. If it be behavioural issues with dogs all the way up to high standard trialling dogs.

12. If you have the same dog again, what will you so different?

The one thing I would definitely do differently with Axels training I would have trained the 'out' command.

13. Is he / she social with people?

Axel is very social with people out of drive, he is very calm and collective. He can be trusted around people and children, until I give him the word and the dog completely changes and its time for work.

14. Any funny stories you want to share?

N/A.

15. If you can change 1 thing about the dog, what would it be?

The one thing I would change about Axel if I could but I know I can't is for him to be slightly bigger and heavier in weight.

16. How was the dog like when he/ she as a puppy?

Axel as a puppy was your typical malinois puppy. He was always on the go, always wanted to bite everything that moved. He would be in high drive after it. To be fair I miss the days of him being a puppy, he was a good little character. I knew when I got him I had a good dog on my hands, and what a good dog he has turned out to be.

17. How was he / she like as he / she matured?

The dog was still overdriven but a lot more focused now he has matured.

18. How are the dog's litter mates?

What I have heard about Axel's litter mates is that they are all progressing well and working at different levels.

19. Is he / she social with other dogs?

Axel is very good around dogs, but he will not tolerate dominant dogs as he is quite dominant himself.

20. Does the dog live in a house or a kennel?

Axel has lived in a kennel all his life,

Dog 80 – Pharoah (BRN36375)

Owner: Tai Nero

1. How is he / she at home, out of work?

He's good when he's not working. He stays in the house.

2. Describe his or her character with 5 words..

Determine, evil, fast, smart and fearless.

3. What is his / her best quality?

He's always willing, he will not stop, and you can count on him to complete a task.

4. What is his / her least desirable attribute?

He hates obedience unless there's some type of conflict or biting involved.

5. Is he / she one of your favourite dogs of all time?

Absolutely one of my favorites!

6. What is his / her favourite activity?

His favorite activity is bitework!

7. What is his / her biggest achievements?

His first biggest achievement was being the youngest Malinois to earn a PSA PDC Suit. He just turned 6 months old 3 day prior. This year 2020 he earned one of the hardest titles The APPDA Level 3.

8. Was he / she difficult to train?

He fit right into my program, definitely my type of dog. In the wrong hands he would have hurt someone.

9. What's your favourite offspring of his / her?

I haven't bred him yet.

10. How heavy was or is he / she?

N/A.

11. Where is your training club and decoys who helped him / her?

My club is in New York (Allstars Working Dogs APPDA) Pharaoh has been in front of some of the best decoys and trainers starting with Carlos Colon, Garvin Hercules, Jose Iglesias, James Guillory, Anthony Quartieri, Matt Rogers, Mark Banks, Nic Tolson, Stephane Hubert, Charlie Randolph, Dez Lynch, Andre Carmichael, Jovan Colon, Orbett Blagmon Jr, Robert Pruna, Mell Pritchett, Evan Griggs, Dale Anderson Christian Stickney, Eric Konosky, and Kellen David.

12. If you have the same dog again, what will you so different?

I would do everything the same. Same team, same training.

13. Is he / she social with people?

He's social, not friendly. I can bring him to public, crowded events or areas and he's fine. Just don't reach for him but I'm a responsible owner and always aware of my surroundings with him.

14. Any funny stories you want to share?

N/A.

15. If you can change 1 thing about the dog, what would it be?

I wouldn't change NOTHING! He is who he is and it worked for me.

16. How was the dog like when he/ she as a puppy?

He was an evil puppy, over confident and fearless. Wanting to kill everyone but always willing to please.

17. How was he / she like as he / she matured?

As an adult he's the same dog just with control.

18. How are the dog's litter mates?

N/A.

19. Is he / she social with other dogs?

Dogs only do what you allow them to do. He's cool because he has no choice if he can make a decision it will be to fight anything and everyone.

20. Does the dog live in a house or a kennel?

He lives in the house with me. Why have a dog like this and keep him locked up.

Dog 81 - Max of Mumbai United

Owner: Chetan J Chauhan and trainer: Rajender Chauhan (Bunty)

1. How is he / she at home, out of work?

Max is usually very calm and social at home, he plays with my kids and lives happily. He is good with my pet Shih Tzu. He is just a lovely dog.

2. Describe his or her character with 5 words..

Crazy drives, intensity, fearlessness, he is always ready to please and his owner love, endorphin junkie.

3. What is his / her best quality?

His best quality is he is the same everywhere you just tell him and he is ready for work, his eagerness to please, training is one of the best things about him. The level of drive he has perfectly matches mine. I believe he is my perfect match.

4. What is his / her least desirable attribute?

I just like everything about him, he is one of a kind, there is nothing in him that is not undesirable, he is just perfect.

5. Is he / she one of your favourite dogs of all time?

He is my best dog ever. I fear I will not get a dog like him ever again in my life. I have his son with me who is growing and becoming like him but Max has some different kind of drive and craziness.

6. What is his / her favourite activity?

He just loves to bite decoys, he literally lives for it, he is ready to bite anyone, anytime and anywhere. He just loves to bite.

7. What is his / her biggest achievements?

We did his PDC in only 52 days. He is a PSA 1 dog and will be attempting PSA 2 this season but still I believe he is the only dog I know who did a PDC in 52 days of training. He came to me when he was 9 months old and he didn't have any prior foundation of the exercises and it was a huge challenge to me too but we succeeded with a lot of hardwork and his drives helped me alot. We used to train him 3 times a day at that time and he did it.

8. Was he / she difficult to train?

Yes he was quite a difficult dog because of very limited time I had to work very hard on him and when he came to me he was an out of control drive maniac, he bit me many times during his initial months because he used to get out of control in drives.

9. What's your favourite offspring of his / her?

His son Ceaser (who is still with me) and daugther Storm. These two are littermates from our brood bitch Kimmy. Max is a very consistent producer, he has never produced a low drive puppy but this combo he has with Kimmy is special and also because both these pups Ceaser and Storm have grown in front of me, I have a special place for them in my heart.

10. How heavy was or is he / she?

He is approx 30 kg, a very fast dog with super stamina and a courageous heart.

11. Where is your training club and decoys who helped him / her?

My training club is Wolfmaster k9, located in Faridabad, Haryana, India. We are a PSA club and our main decoys who have helped him grow are Nikhil Kumar, Raju and Deepak Chauhan.

12. If you have the same dog again, what will you so different?

If I ever get this kind of dog again in my life I would like to train him from puppyhood and do proper foundation. He could have become a better dog. He does get out of control at times because of him not having proper foundation but still he is my favourite, just like his son is a foundation trained dog and he is more intelligent, more controllable and with super intensity. He is going to be a very good scoring dog in future for sure.

13. Is he / she social with people?

Yes Max is a very social dog. He can play ball with the same decoy once he is out of the suit. People here love him the most, he is good with children. He helps us in socialising our pet client dogs and he has not misbehaved even a single time with anyone.

14. Any funny stories you want to share?

No, don't remember anything he has done which was funny.

15. If you can change 1 thing about the dog, what would it be?

It would be his hyper activeness, he does become a problem when teaching him something new and he gets too excited and because of his drive and intensity he always breaks plastic objects when he is told to retrieve them.

16. How was the dog like when he/ she as a puppy?

He came to me when he was 9 month old already so I never got to see his puppyhood.

17. How was he / she like as he / she matured?

He is a mature dog now he behaves very maturely in training as well as in daily life.

18. How are the dog's litter mates?

No information about any of his littermates.

19. Is he / she social with other dogs?

Yes he is very social with dogs.

20. Does the dog live in a house or a kennel?

He stays in my house and kennel and is comfortable in both the conditions.

Dog 82 - Lorockmor Chloe (BRN27407)

Owner: Ian Morgan

1. How is he / she at home, out of work?

At home out of work Chloe is quite relaxed and chilled, she enjoys walks and is quite playful with the other dogs, running and chasing one another around.

2. Describe his or her character with 5 words..

Strong, intent, clear, tough and focused.

3. What is his / her best quality?

Chloe has many qualities such as her looks, her structure, her focus, power, natural bite mechanics, clear head, willingness to work and great nerve. She's everyone's dream female.

4. What is his / her least desirable attribute?

The worst thing about her is she chews the hair on her tail when in season.

5. Is he / she one of your favourite dogs of all time?

Chloe is undoubtedly one of my favourite dogs I've ever owned and I've owned a lot of dogs but she's right at the top of the list.

6. What is his / her favourite activity?

Chloe's favourite activities are bitework, playing ball and chasing her buddies round the fields.

7. What is his / her biggest achievements?

Chloe has won several avd events mostly in Germany as she always has pups around the time of the UK event. She has won long send competitions and the highest level class night trials.

8. Was he / she difficult to train?

She was very easy to train, a dog with super natural ability.

9. What's your favourite offspring of his / her?

Chloe has been a great producer but my favourite offspring has to be Mensa.

10. How heavy was or is he / she?

34kg.

11. Where is your training club and decoys who helped him / her?

My training club is Lorockmor working dogs which has great facilities and super decoys Paul Harding, Asa Wright, Laurie Stanley, Will Holmes, Dalton Rush have all helped with Chloe's progress over the years.

12. If you have the same dog again, what will you so different?

If I had Chloe again I'd train more with her, maybe in a sport like the KNPV program.

13. Is he / she social with people?

She can be social but has also had an unprovoked live bite also.

14. Any funny stories you want to share?

There was one time I had some men working at my house, I'd taken Chloe for a walk, I wasn't concentrating just walking along looking at my phone as you do. when I looked up, I thought to myself where has she gone to? I hear a few seconds later one of the men (Kevin) shouting my name! As I ran up towards him I could see Chloe was latched onto his thigh, full mouth bite trying to drive in and Kevin was there holding her collar to try to stop her and get her off! Luckily Kevin is a good guy and didn't cause any trouble over it, a trip to the hospital and everything was ok.

15. If you can change 1 thing about the dog, what would it be?

I would not change a single thing about her, she's perfect.

16. How was the dog like when he/ she as a puppy?

She arrived from Holland as a 16 week old puppy along with two others but straight away she stood out head and shoulders above the other two. She was such a natural it was unbelievable, no matter what I asked of her she could do it and do it well.

18. How are the dog's litter mates?

Unfortunately I don't know anything about any of her litter mates.

19. Is he / she social with other dogs?

She is social with most other dogs, there's just the odd one or two she doesn't get on with but I think that's more their fault than hers.

20. Does the dog live in a house or a kennel?

Chloe lives outside in the kennel block.

Dog 83 - Lorockmor Dax (BRN37897)

Owner: Ian Morgan

1. How is he / she at home, out of work?

Dax is never out of work, I honestly have never come across a dog like him! He is constantly looking to do bitework, the dog is obsessed.

2. Describe his or her character with 5 words..

Mental, stubborn, hard headed, nightmare and a dickhead.

3. What is his / her best quality?

His best quality is his want for work, the dog just lives for it he thinks of nothing else.

4. What is his / her least desirable attribute?

He does not listen or learn, I've never known a dog like him.

5. Is he / she one of your favourite dogs of all time?

We have a love-hate relationship. I love his hardiness and heart but I hate the fact that he never switches off.

6. What is his / her favourite activity?

Bite bite bite he lives for it!

7. What is his / her biggest achievements?

Only ever trialled him once and he got 2nd place in Avd gold class, the toughest one I think I've ever seen.

8. Was he / she difficult to train?

Extremely difficult to try and get control of him, he's a dog that will come back at you if you punish him.

9. What's your favourite offspring of his / her?

All his offspring are too young to say.

10. How heavy was or is he / she?

42 kg.

11. Where is your training club and decoys who helped him / her?

My club is Lorockmor working dogs, Paul Harding has done most of the work with Dax.

12. If you have the same dog again, what will you so different?

I didn't get him until he was two and a half years old, I would have loved to have him as a pup.

13. Is he / she social with people?

No he's not a social dog, it took me three weeks to get him to stop trying to bite me when I bought him.

14. Any funny stories you want to share?

I was working him on a female decoy once and the lead snapped and he knocked her to the floor. Luckily he was clean and no one was hurt.

15. If you can change 1 thing about the dog, what would it be?

If I could change anything it would be that he had an off switch and I wish he'd just relax and be a normal dog every now and then.

16. How was the dog like when he/ she as a puppy?

I don't know what he was like as a puppy.

17. How was he / she like as he / she matured?

He's a big strong powerful dog that you don't want to get on the wrong side of.

18. How are the dog's litter mates?

From what I hear and what I have seen his litter mates are very good, he's siblings seem very consistent.

19. Is he / she social with other dogs?

He is lovely and social with females but not males.

20. Does the dog live in a house or a kennel?

He lives outside in the kennel block.

Dog 84 - Ren Maria (BRN31404)

Owner: Holly Benitez

1. How is he / she at home, out of work?

VAt home she's pretty good. She splits her day half the time between my kitchen and the garden. She's quiet and clean inside. Goes outside around 9 am and is in and out until bedtime at 10 pm. You won't hear her after that

2. Describe his or her character with 5 words..

She's highly motivated, happy and violent.

3. What is his / her best quality?

I'd say her biting mechanics and grip as well as her courage. I'm told she bites hard and is a bit intimidating (but fun)!

4. What is his / her least desirable attribute?

She can be impulsive in drive if not well managed. She's not a bad dog who wants to be in trouble, so if set up correctly she will most times make the correct decisions. But I can say I have decided to eat some points in precision so as to drive her the way I want. She's a pretty external dog so her motivation or level of stimulation is manifested in some sort of "chant to satan". This happens mostly when she knows there's a chance to bite. I argued with myself for months about how much she was aware of and how much just comes along for the ride once she hits a certain level of stimulation. A lot of it is involuntary and if I correct her she may quieten a bit, but don't be fooled she's just been knocked down temporarily in excitement and is being a bit careful (well as careful as Ren can be). She's not a dog that gets her feelings hurt easily or takes things personally. She's never redirected or dropped her tail once.

The sound of her on deck is a steady deep "Ra ra ra Raaa", and if i could translate it I'm sure it's probably "who who who"!!

5. Is he / she one of your favourite dogs of all time?

Yes, most definitely! I'm a breeder. I've owned many dogs! She's the best I've produced and handled. While she's not an easy dog she's fun.

6. What is his / her favourite activity?

Surprisingly she loves going down to a popular tourist rafting location (Ocoee river). She will happily take pets from random river hippies. Then of course biting! Thank God she hasn't decided to combine the two on her own yet! I'd feel terrible if she smashed some river rat (that's what we call guides and hard-core river folks). She also loves hiking and recognizes the road to the trail and will sing about it until we park!

7. What is his / her biggest achievements?

She's still young, just 3 as of September 21st. She's had 2 litters. The first is an outcross into some Pegge lines. As a breeder I wanted to see how strong she could be as a producer. And thankfully I can report they came out pretty consistent and nice. She has 7 week old puppies as I write this. She is soon to be back training for her PSA 1. She earned her PSA PDC in good style at The PSA Midwest Regionals. She was a crowd favorite I'm told. She's also titled in dock diving for fun and some other temperament certs.

8. Was he / she difficult to train?

She's always been a super operant and easily motivated smart dog from a wee puppy. Super food drive and prey drive to spare and some nice aggression in there too. She's not the easiest dog to push into defense so she operates mostly in prey (but I have no doubt if worse came to worst she'd take some damage and do fine). I've always had those attributes on my side to manipulate. She's naturally social, open and pretty reckless. We spent 6 months teaching her to stop smashing jumps, barriers and walls. But touching on what I said earlier, control is her struggle. And mine it's our challenge. I've built a good, fair relationship with her from day one and never had to ask her to out more than once to date. She expects fairness from me. But she is resilient enough to take a unfair correction if I make a mistake without crumbling (I'm only human).

Relationship is how I control her. No it's not all rainbows, but most times she knows "if I do as Holly says i get it again". She accepts my input and never redirects or comes up the leash. I'd never have such a cur in my opinion.

9. What's your favourite offspring of his / her?

Favorite offspring: I'd have to mention "Habby" owned by Tarra Mathews-Wheeler. She's a little mini Ren in a lot of ways. Tarra intends to compete in PSA. There were actually 2 super females off that litter, one is out west training for dual. Currently Ren has a litter off "Evil" from the Netherlands. This is linebreeding and I have high hopes.

10. How heavy was or is he / she?

Ren has been referred to as a "shemale" often. She sits at a fit 74 pounds with a large head and tall well muscled body and piercing light colored eyes. Most folks who saw her trial including the Judge called her "he". She's got some presence to her.

11. Where is your training club and decoys who helped him / her?

I train outside of a conventional "Club". So that's anywhere me and Adrian happen to be. We have a family-like relationship. She's been there since Ren was 5 months old. I was very strict about sticking to 1 decoy only during foundation. I NEVER broke that. Without Adrian Rae (Decoy) and Tracey, our friend we wouldn't be having this conversation. I owe it all to both of them. I'm on the spectrum so let's say I'm a bit quirky. But they kept me and Ren level. I can't count or tell how many days I just held that leash and hoped Tracey was behind me somewhere. She always was! Adrian knew what Ren was when she saw her. She's always taken time to help me harness what I have. I appreciate her more than I can articulate.

12. If you have the same dog again, what will you so different?

I would tell myself to breathe! Maybe walk a little faster. I'd done more capping drills.

13. Is he / she social with people?

She's literally a sweetheart. Loves everyone. Recently she jumped in Adrian's van in her lap. She was so happy! Adrian not so much. Adrian knows the level of violence she can dish.

14. Any funny stories you want to share?

When she was about a year old she mowed me over in front of some elderly people at a public park. I took too long on a phone call that interrupted her chunk it session! She went full speed and hit me in the back! This one lady came over to see if I was okay. She asked "Does she see ok?" To which I embarrassingly had to admit yes but she's impatient!

15. If you can change 1 thing about the dog, what would it be?

N/A.

16. How was the dog like when he/ she as a puppy?

As a puppy she was super fun. Loved learning! She was born a singleton and I bottle raised her in my house from day 1. Every 2 hours I fed her and stimulated her to potty. I actually carried her around like some little pomeranian or toy dog in an oversized purse!

17. How was he / she like as he / she matured?

She began being possessive as soon as she could bite with coordination and would grab my arms and wrap. It was ridiculous! She was happy to go anywhere and wasn't phased by anything.

18. How are the dog's litter mates?

She has no litter mates.

19. Is he / she social with other dogs?

She is social with dogs as long as no one gets stupid. Her best friend is a 4 lbs chihuahua my husband owns.

20. Does the dog live in a house or a kennel?

She lived in my kitchen/ laundry room her entire life. She does spend some daytime out on a cable in my garden. I don't like to have a working dog too acclimated to AC or heating or cooped up either for enrichment purposes.

Dog 85 - Noodle (BRN28914)

Owner: Alan Young

1. How is he / she at home, out of work?

At home she is always 100 mile an hour I think is the best way to describe her. She is very intense in everything she does be it running, playing or cuddling. She is a very alert bitch and misses nothing but a great family guardian and is also very social.

2. Describe his or her character with 5 words..

Intense, fun, forward, loose and determined.

3. What is his / her best quality?

She is a very committed bitch who always puts her all into every challenge. She is very reliable in bitework and works better under pressure than in green field work.

4. What is his / her least desirable attribute?
The least desirable attribute in my opinion would be that she works out obedience patterns quickly and is trial smart, making it difficult to hold onto her in obedience portions of competition. She has the potential to score highly as she

knows the obedience exercises well, but due to the mentioned attributes she often sells herself short.

5. Is he / she one of your favourite dogs of all time?

Yes for sure, I believe it is very hard to get a real good working bitch and she has competed against some of the best in the UK and always leaves me with a smile on my face. She ticks a lot of boxes! She's super fun, social, loveable, hard working and committed in her bitework.

6. What is his / her favourite activity?

She is a very rounded bitch to be honest and loves all activities, she's happy go lucky. But to pick one it would have to be bitework with playing ball a close second. She enjoys pressure and "real" situations as opposed to sport. The more intense the activity, the better for Noodle.

7. What is his / her biggest achievements?

She is a jack of all trades, mainly due to the lack of sports to work towards in N.I. She has achieved:

- PDC and PSA1 (One of the first females in Europe to achieve her PSA1 and qualified for nationals)
- Entry Level APPDA
- ZWP2
- Silver Class A.V.D ev (placing 8th & 4th consecutively)
- Cat 1 Global Ring (score 186 and qualified for nationals)

8. Was he / she difficult to train?

Yes and no. She was always easy in the bitework but difficult in obedience. She never had great food drive as a puppy which is my preferred method to gain clean precise obedience. Her ball drive was always good though so it was used instead but just took longer to brush up behaviours as she is quite high for the ball. Her obedience in bite work is challenging also as she is so committed to the grip and equipment collar smart, which means on trial day she can become a little loose around the decoy and sticky on outs which has cost us a few points over her career.

9. What's your favourite offspring of his / her?

Noodle has been quite challenging when it comes to breeding. We only got 2 pups out of the first litter, my keeper Spires Jaffa who is looking promising and I am looking forward to working and testing this year as she turns 16 months. In her second litter Noodle had 4 pups who are all still very young but again the signs are good and we have our first male pup Spires Mozart (Mozzi) who is really fun and showing a lot of Noodle characteristics so watch this space.

10. How heavy was or is he / she?

Noodle is 32Kg, she is not overly big, but she is quite a long backed bitch.

11. Where is your training club and decoys who helped him / her?

Noodle has been trained by myself from a pup. She has been worked by many decoys and trainers from NI, SOI, England, Canada & USA who have all helped her progress to the dog she is today, thanks to all those involved!

12. If you have the same dog again, what will you so different?

If I were to start again, I would probably have balanced her training more as a puppy with less frustration in the early months as this I believe has caused some conflict with obedience in later years. However I have to admit I love the intensity the frustration has delivered.

13. Is he / she social with people?

Yes! She is very social and is an intense cuddler, it is actually annoying sometimes. She loves attention and getting petted regardless of who from. Even after bitework once she has switched off, she will happily socialize with those around.

14. Any funny stories you want to share?

Noodle as an 8 or 10 week pup was the passenger in a car crash, she was seatbelted into the back seat, the car was a write off but Noodle sat happy as larry in the back and hopped out after and ran around as if nothing had happened. She even got to sit in the police car to warm up while they took statements. She also a few weeks later was out running beside the quad and got one of her legs ran over and again bounced up as if nothing had happened. A cat with 9 lives wouldn't have a look in!

15. If you can change 1 thing about the dog, what would it be?

If there was one thing I could add it would be enhanced food drive as a puppy, that would have made her training much easier and faster..

16. How was the dog like when he/ she as a puppy?

Absolutely crazy! I don't think I saw her sleep until she was 6 months old. She was intense, fun, social, bitey and into all the badness she could find.

17. How was he / she like as he / she matured?

Pretty much the same! Still crazy, mischievous, intense and fun thankfully! As she matured a lot of the play has remained but she has a civil side which has developed well since her first litter. Although she is very social, she is still very much a one man dog.

18. How are the dog's litter mates?

Really good, the other two siblings I have seen and worked are very consistent and good family guardians.

19. Is he / she social with other dogs?

She is social and is my go to bitch for teaching puppies how to play and socialise. She teaches them how to interact whilst putting them in their place if they get too much.

Although she is social she can be intense in her play and sometimes this can be intimidating for other dogs.

20. Does the dog live in a house or a kennel?

Both, we have a few dogs so they take turns to be in the house or outside. In the house she is a strong guardian and loves to be pampered. Outside she retains her guarding instincts and is generally a good clean quiet dog unless disturbed.

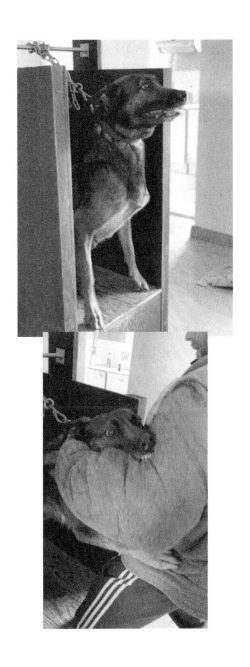

Dog 86 - Antik von den brennenden Herzen
(VDH05/1470077)

Owner: Arne Pohlmeyer

1. How is he / she at home, out of work?

Antik was always a friendly and stable family dog. From the beginning she was confident and safe with children and friends of the family. However, it was more pleasant to keep her mainly outside of the house as she was a bit too annoying in the house. Antik did not damage anything in the house and was never a nervous barker or anything like that. Due to her high "will to please" she wanted to be around her humans all the time and always offered her willingness to work. For example, as soon as I got up from the couch she got up immediately and wanted to work. In the kennel she had a lot more peace and quiet than in the house. You could take Antik with you everywhere, it never showed even the slightest environmental problem. She was so open and stable as I had hardly seen in any other dog. Nothing made her nervous or scared. Whether you were out and about with her in the big city or in the forest, she was always docile.

2. Describe his or her character with 5 words..

Will to please, high drive, bravery, intelligence and lovable.

3. What is his / her best quality?

Antik had an extremely high prey drive without becoming thoughtless. She was extremely intelligent and capable of learning. Her "will to please" was very pronounced. She always wanted to please me and make me happy. Her environmental safety and courage were legendary. In addition to her impressive performance of obedience, I must mention her high speed, jumping ability and her spectacular "long sends". Antik was a very enduring dog who consistently performed evenly. Not a dog that had quickly shot its gunpowder but one that stable and consistently delivered the same.

4. What is his / her least desirable attribute?

She hardly had any real flaws, the only thing I would have mentioned was that she couldn't relax well in the house because she was constantly waiting for work. She caught and retrieved one of my hunting terriers which was also a problem.

5. Is he / she one of your favourite dogs of all time?

Definitely! I've never had a comparable dog again. Not one who could be led so well. She has always made me happy and always wanted to make me happy. There was hardly any dog who was as constant as she was.

6. What is his / her favourite activity?

Obedience training, protection training mainly in the AVD Freestyle ring sport type. But she also enjoyed cycling, ball games and free forms of agility.

7. What is his / her biggest achievements?

Antik has won uncountable trophies for night trials, long sends, ring face attacks, obedience competitions and things like that. It should also be noted that she has also made IPO-Sports. I took her to an exam in the IPO dog sport where she received the maximum score of 100 points in the protection part. It almost never happens, but her performance was flawless.

8. Was he / she difficult to train?

Antik was very easy to train. The centre of her life was the interest to work and to learn something from me. A real team player. For me much more a 100% real Malinois than the dogs you often see today.

9. What's your favourite offspring of his / her?

A'Patrasch from the Lönshütte, Biene von der Lönsmeute (aka Diestel) & Bang Bang from the Lönshütte (aka Axel).

10. How heavy was or is he / she?

Approx. 28kg.

11. Where is your training club and decoys who helped him / her?

AVD e. V. of course and SV e. V. - all the decoys who helped were trained and built up by myself.

12. If you have the same dog again, what will you so different?

I wouldn't do anything else with Antik, except maybe to show her that it is not okay to retrieve terriers from the beginning.

13. Is he / she social with people?

Social to friendly or neutral people, but was able to go quickly into civil protection when it was needed.

14. Any funny stories you want to share?

No fun stories but a lot of lovely memories but this will stay in my head and in my heart.

15. If you can change 1 thing about the dog, what would it be?

The same as with all dogs: even better grips, I'm almost never satisfied with that. The grips can still be coarser and harsher for me, there is no upper limit.

16. How was the dog like when he/ she as a puppy?

I got her as a young dog, but by then she wasn't a real puppy anymore. You couldn't really notice a lot of developmental changes in her, one of the dogs that you can call "born ready".

17. How was he / she like as he / she matured?

Constant, reliable, persistent and always ready.

18. How are the dog's litter mates?

Some did IPO sports, but I don't really have contact with the owners. I cannot judge correctly.

19. Is he / she social with other dogs?

Was not openly aggressive and showed good behaviour, but it was too dangerous to let her play with stranger dogs.

20. Does the dog live in a house or a kennel?

As I said above, she lived with a lot of family contact but almost always slept in the kennel.

Dog 87 - Thekla vom Diensthundezwinger Bielefeld

Owner: Arne Pohlmeyer

1. How is he / she at home, out of work?

Thekla was very calm and inconspicuous in the house, but it was hardly possible to keep the dog free in the house, as the danger was too great that a stranger might come into contact with her. All strangers were always attacked immediately by her. That's why I had Thekla either in the kennel or in a large stable box in the house.

2. Describe his or her character with 5 words..

Ready for defense at any time and in any situation, the dog was always awake, uncompromising forward drive, manhunter and adorable.

3. What is his / her best quality?

Thekla was a serious dog through and through. For her strangers were nothing more than biting-objects. She was one of the best security service dogs I have ever seen. Perhaps that she almost never tended to bark but rather to lurk. This behaviour can of course lead to "live bites" more quickly in the official area, as little warning was visible to strangers. Thekla did not freak out when she saw strangers, but as soon as you were within reach that she could reach you, she immediately bit. Thekla's teeth were like a magnet for strangers. Outside of capable dog handler hands, it would have ended up as a dangerous problem dog in the general opinion. A real personal protection dog who always needed a muzzle as security for other people. And the muzzle did not make her less defensive either. Without exaggeration, there were several people who got too close to me or the dog and paid for it with bruised and even broken ribs.

4. What is his / her least desirable attribute?

For normal people, Thekla certainly had a lot of faults or would have been completely impracticable. But for an experienced dog man she was a gifted guard dog and an incorruptible defender.

But I must mention at this point that she was very bad when traveling. When I took Thekla with me for a weekend, she often peed, ate and drank again only when she got home. Outside of my premises, she was too much in work mode that she completely ignored basic needs.

5. Is he / she one of your favourite dogs of all time?

Yes absolutely! Even if it can be very stressful to own such a dog, safety precautions had to be taken constantly. In terms of reliable protection, I have hardly seen an equivalent dog.

6. What is his / her favourite activity?

Bite!

7. What is his / her biggest achievements?

Thekla has received a lot of trophies for winning night exercises. She has also won the very hard gold class of the AVD e. V. several times!

8. Was he / she difficult to train?

Thekla did what she did, for a Malinois she wasn't much interested in education. Although she played a little with me, everything was not worth mentioning. What she did and loved was protection work or, in a nutshell, "people bite".

9. What's your favourite offspring of his / her?

I often thought about breeding with her. There were many inquiries. But I never did! Since I hardly trusted anyone to lead and keep such dogs. And I didn't want to breed dogs that would later cause accidents out of respect for all good dog people, as it can throw a bad light on all protection dog friends.

10. How heavy was or is he / she?

Approx. 30kg

11. Where is your training club and decoys who helped him / her?

AVD e. V. - all the decoys who helped were trained and built up by me. But to be honest the dog was used often for protection competitions but was not really trained.

12. If you have the same dog again, what will you so different?

I would pay a lot to have the same dog again, but then I would take it over when it was still a puppy, the younger the better - for this type of dog.

13. Is he / she social with people?

NO! The exact opposite, except for your own family.

14. Any funny stories you want to share?

No fun stories, only serious stories.

15. If you can change 1 thing about the dog, what would it be?

More 'will to please' in play situations and, as always with all dogs, even better grips.

16. How was the dog like when he/ she as a puppy?

I got her as an adult dog. The previous owner was a police dog handler who was severely bitten by another service dog and was therefore released from duty. This experienced dog handler came completely unprepared, at an AVD event with Thekla and won the gold class of the night exercise. Then I informed him that the bitch had impressed me very much. Three weeks later my phone rang. He called me and asked if I wanted to take over the dog because he hardly had any idea who could lead and hold the dog and he had to hand it over. I immediately agreed. A few days later I had Thekla at home with me. I had to leave the muzzle on the dog for a whole week because it took a long time before she accepted me.

17. How was he / she like as he / she matured?

Absolutely reliable, always ready.

18. How are the dog's litter mates?

I saw only some litter mates done some IPO Sports on the internet, some did some fullsuit work, but I had no contact with the owners.

19. Is he / she social with other dogs?

Not dog friendly but also not overly aggressive.

20. Does the dog live in a house or a kennel?

In the kennel and in the house but if I was not directly in the same room as her, I put her in a safe kennel box with enough space of course. I was always worried that the dog might break out due to an accident and seriously injure someone, which would certainly have happened if she had seen a stranger.

Dog 88 - K9 Denny (retired)

Owner and handler: Sgt. Rob Avedisian (retired) of the Camden County Sheriff's Office Georgia, USA

He was then handpicked by Bill Heiser from Southern Coast K9 (SCK9). Denny was then flown to Florida where he would begin his explosive detection and apprehension training at SCK9. I then went down to SCK9 and tested 5 different K9s. At that time, I picked K9 Denny to be my partner. His drive was through the roof and his focus on the training aid was remarkable.

I then brought K9 Denny home and we spent about a month doing nothing but bonding together (walks, play, feed, fetch, etc.). We then went to school together for two months of explosive odor detection (EOD) and apprehension training. Our EOD school was put on by the Georgia Emergency Management Agency (GEMA) hosted by the Chatham County Sheriff's Office in Savannah. K-9 Denny graduated school imprinted on 27 different explosive odors. Through his career he was certified through the NNDDA, GEMA, ATF and went to school for advanced explosive handling with the USPCA hosted by the Boston Police Department.

Our 6 ½ years working together we were deployed over 570 times doing various things like, explosive safety sweeps, search for weapons and bomb threats making up most of what K9 Denny did. K-9 protected our children from bomb threats and doing sweeps at our local school events where mass gatherings would happen. K9 Denny also did VIP protection details for; Dalai Lama, 4 US presidents, 2 vice presidents, 27th Presiding Bishop of the US (Bishop Curry) who participated in the royal wedding, there is some UK info for ya lol, Speaker of the house Paul Ryan and John Bohner, Mark Zuckerberg, 15 different governors and many numerous foreign dignitaries. He also did explosive sweeps for NASCAR at Atlanta Motor Speedway, the Georgia Dome and Mercedes Benz Stadium for Atlanta Falcons, Atlanta United, Garth Brooks, Monster Truck, Motocross, music concerts and college football. K9 Denny was also handpicked by GEMA to be only one of eight K9s out of 208 to be inside the stadium during the 2018 Super Bowl and trusted to keep one of the most attended and watched events safe. K9 Denny tracked down numerous weapons that were thrown during pursuits and sometimes in the swamp where they never would have been recovered if it wasn't for his remarkable nose.

K9 Denny was also deployed to find explosives that had been stolen and hidden with possible booby traps. After an entire neighborhood was evacuated, his nose was trusted to lead the way for the Explosive Ordnance Disposal Technicians and make sure that no one would get hurt. K9 Denny searched 5 vehicles, outside the perimeter of a house, front yard, back yard, and two sheds. K-9 Denny ended up alerting to the floor of one of the sheds. EOD Techs ended up digging a foot and a half in the ground when they found 60 pounds of C2 Sheet explosives, blasting caps, Detonation cord, 40 MM grenades and over 60 cans of ammunition. That day K9 Denny went down in Georgia history for finding the largest buried cache of explosives ever found by a K9.

1. How is he / she at home, out of work?

When K9 Denny is at home he is just one of the family. He plays with my daughter, wife and my other dogs just like any other dog. When he goes to work I take his house collar off and put on his work collar. Once that happens he knows its game time and he becomes K9 Denny instead of just Denny.

2. Describe his or her character with 5 words..

Partner, Best Friend, and family member.

3. What is his / her best quality?

Denny's best qualities are his relentless drive and the fact he can go from apprehension to detection mode and then to getting pet by the kids at the schools just like throwing a light switch.

4. What is his / her least desirable attribute?

He won't give his Kong back after being rewarded.

5. Is he / she one of your favourite dogs of all time?

I've had dogs my whole life; I could never single one out. He is my favorite bomb dog that I ever had.

6. What is his / her favourite activity?

He loves to work and get that reward and praise.

7. What is his / her biggest achievements?

Largest buried find in Georgia History.

8. Was he / she difficult to train?

Denny trained me, I didn't train him. He made me look good.

9. What's your favourite offspring of his / her?

K9 Denny has been fixed and did not sire any pups.

10. How heavy was or is he / she?

K9 Denny's working weight was 68 pounds.

11. Where is your training club and decoys who helped him / her?

K9 Denny was trained and or certified at Southern Coast K9, GEMA, NNDDA, USPCA and the ATF.

12. If you have the same dog again, what will you so different?

I wouldn't change anything except maybe getting his kong back a little easier (handler's fault).

13. Is he / she social with people?

K9 Denny was and is amazing with people he goes to schools, senior citizen care homes and plays with my kid.

14. Any funny stories you want to share?

During training one time while doing detection work K9 Denny noticed I had his Kong with a rope in it through my belt behind me. Me not paying attention like I should have (bad handler) he went after the kong and when he did, he got the kong and the rope. So now he has the Kong in his mouth behind me and as I said before he does not like to out. So he is pulling me around the training area and with each tug my pants are falling down and down further. Of course all the other handlers are being handlers and are laughing and not helping. I couldn't be mad because I was laughing too. Eventually he re-gripped and the rope part came out of his mouth and he ran away with his trophy the Kong in his mouth and me a little less dressed.

15. If you can change 1 thing about the dog, what would it be?

The only thing I would change was for him to live longer.

16. How was the dog like when he/ she as a puppy?

He was born in Germany and I didn't meet him until he was almost 2.

17. How was he / she like as he / she matured?

As he got older the only thing that changed was his muzzle got some grey in it.

18. How are the dog's litter mates?

I have no idea where his litter mates ended up.

19. Is he / she social with other dogs?

K9 Denny does not like other alpha male dogs, however he does love the ladies, a lot.

20. Does the dog live in a house or a kennel?

He lives in the house just like every other family member. I have been very fortunate that all of my working K9s know the difference between home and work.

I was very lucky to have K-9 Denny as my EOD K-9. I also retired with him in August 2020.

Dog 89 - Samson

Owner: Aidan Miller

1. How is he / she at home, out of work?

Out of work Samson has been brought up in the house similar to how a pet dog would be. He has been brought up around babies, children and visitors. Typical to a high drive Malinois it wasn't easy to house train him but with persistence he became a loving member of the family that was easy to manage in the house I believe this is what created a strong bond and trusting relationship.

2. Describe his or her character with 5 words..

Loving, tenacious, courageous, balanced and educational.

3. What is his / her best quality?

His best quality is his forgivingness. As a working dog to a first time working dog owner Samson was able to take my mistakes and easily accept correctional training quickly without long lasting damage. Where most dogs would be "broken" , Samson would always come out the other end a stronger dog regardless of my naivety and lack of experience.

4. What is his / her least desirable attribute?

Samsons least desirable quality is what comes as a result of my own training. Although trained to be social, Samson does not see a threat from passive threats and strangers; this has been a problem in some of the working situations we have been placed in on the streets dealing with some of Birmingham's most undesirables.

5. Is he / she one of your favourite dogs of all time?

Samson will always be my favourite unreplaceable dog of all time not because of his ability to work or any characteristics he has displayed over the past three years but purely down to what he has done for my family. When I first bought Samson I was a depressed self-absorbed young man that had no direction or purpose. Owning him taught me focus and a sense of meaning through training. It also gave me the confidence to take a giant leap and launch my own business revolving solely around General Purpose Security Dogs. Samson has not only changed my life but also changed the life of my family.

6. What is his / her favourite activity?

Samson is a lover of swimming that will swim until he is recalled.

7. What is his / her biggest achievements?

Samson is currently at his prime but some of his biggest achievements are winning Defend & Pursue Level 3 in 2019 along with winning multiple obedience trophies. Some of his biggest achievements come without reward or trophies in the workplace. Working on one of Birmingham's biggest arenas Samson was called in with me to restore order to a volatile crowd. Having to walk into a concert with a chest rattling base and thousands of people, Samson was able to control a crowd under extreme environmental pressure and multiple hostile males without taking a backwards step. This was the moment that I realised that Samson was more than just a sports dog.

8. Was he / she difficult to train?

Samson was an easy dog to train. Unlike a lot of the working Malinois Samson's genetics weren't as strong as you would normally want from a puppy almost everything with him was trained and enforced.

9. What's your favourite offspring of his / her?

I have yet to stud Samson out.

10. How heavy was or is he / she?

Samson at a good weight in the summer months is 35kg.

11. Where is your training club and decoys who helped him / her?

Samson has pretty much trained exclusively at Lorockmor working dogs with our trainer being Ian Morgan. His regular decoys have been Paul Harding, Asa Wright and Laurie Stanley all bringing different pros and approaches.

12. If you have the same dog again, what will you so different?

If I was to have the same dog again the only thing I would change is my own approach to training being more knowledgeable id be able to cut out the mistakes I made e.g. corrections and reward timings.

13. Is he / she social with people?

Samson is social to the point I can walk him through large crowds and have him free roaming in almost all situations.

14. Any funny stories you want to share?

There are many funny stories normally relating to Samson that make me look foolish. Samson once jumped up at me in excitement and knocked me out cold but the funniest story which I believe is still documented through a Muzmuztv live stream of Defend and Pursue 2017 trial in Wales. Samson was entered into the long send competition with Dalton Rush as the decoy. To the right hand side of the venue was a lake around 400m in diameter. I sent Samson while he was showing intent and focus on the decoy. Samson ran full pelt towards the decoy and at the last minute changed course and decided he wanted to go for a swim. He spent 30 minutes swimming in the lake without anybody including myself able to recall him. After about 20 minutes the decision was made that I had to go in and get him. The water was cold, dirty and muddy under the surface. I then proceeded to play cat and mouse with him in the water for another 10 or so minutes. He made up for it by placing well in the competition I believe 3rd.

15. If you can change 1 thing about the dog, what would it be?

If I could change one thing about Samson it would be his lifespan. I would increase it as it's going to be a dark day when he passes.

16. How was the dog like when he/ she as a puppy?

As a puppy he was playful, attentive, following me everywhere.

17. How was he / she like as he / she matured?

As he has matured as a product of his environment he has become a reliable serious GP dog that I trust 100% to do the job.

18. How are the dog's litter mates?

Unfortunately I was unable to keep up with his litter mates as the breeder hadn't had feedback.

19. Is he / she social with other dogs?

Samson is socially accepting of other dogs but does not tolerate playful behaviours.

20. Does the dog live in a house or a kennel?

Samson has spent the majority of his life in the house just fine but to offer him a better quality of life he has been transferred to a larger run and kennel outdoors.

Dog 90 - Djaiko (Big Jake) (BRN16949)

Owner: Maynard Pease

Djaiko is one of the strongest dogs to title in the KNPV program. He is very well known throughout the world for his extreme crushing, hard full pushing grips.

If I was asked to describe Djaiko in one word I would say "Extreme". Not only is he one of the strongest dogs we've ever seen but he's also a consistent and proven producer with one of the top producing pedigrees. Djaiko has perfect hips, back and elbows. He has an extremely dominant temperament, with natural aggression but still "clear-headed".

Djaiko drive, courage, and power is something you can't explain. We have never seen it in any other dog! Djaiko's frontal attacks are fast and violent. His grip is very impressive and punishing to the decoy. During his PH I trial in 2012, Djaiko put the decoy into hospital, from a leg bite so powerful it went through the suit. Djaiko's searching, hunt and retrieve drives are the most intense we have ever seen. He is a complete working dog, a true asset to any "work dog" breeding program.

Djaiko

Dog 91 – Max (BRN33786)

Owner: Tini van der Doelen

Max was bred by G. Heinhuis (Born October 10, 2012) and purchased as a puppy by Bert Doeze Jager. Bert trained Max within the KNPV program, and a few months before certification Max was injured. After a stick attack he went lame in one leg. Max was put on rest several different times to give him a chance to heal and possibly still be able to work, however, each time returning to work he would start going lame in that leg again. It was then discovered that he had torn a tendon in his leg and would not be able to work at all anymore. At this point, Bert gave Tini a call and Tini took Max.

To this day, Max still lives with Tini and shares a lot of the same characteristics as his father (Charlie). Max is a social dog. You can be around him and he will be friendly towards you. However, in the instance where he is jumping up on you, you can pet him a bit, all is ok, but if you try to shove him away, he will not accept that. In a way, a bit of a dominant type.

He, just like his father, is a one man's dog and very loyal. Max is always right beside Tini. If Tini has to go pull a trailer with the tractor down the road, Max is right there, jumps up on the tractor or trailer and is ready to ride along. He is always ready for anything. Always right beside you, the type of thing that is natural to a dog, not something that you train.

Dog 92 - Serious Black (BRN30625)

Owner: Tyler Bryan

1. How is he / she at home, out of work?

Serious outside of work is a very loving and affectionate dog. We refer to him as the 'nanny' dog of our house. He's quick to show pups right from wrong and also looks after the rest of our pack with pride.

2. Describe his or her character with 5 words..

Serious' character in 5 words would be brave, willing, loving, trustworthy & loyal without a doubt.

3. What is his / her best quality?

Serious' best quality is that he adapts to any situation in any environment at any time without fail. He is a very committed dog no matter what is thrown his way. No matter if it's pressure from a decoy or myself, he never fails to disappoint.

4. What is his / her least desirable attribute?

Serious' most undesirable trait is his constant need to spin in circles when excited. Also, when he was a younger dog, he'd lock up and not bark whilst in prey drive, partly I am to blame for not asking for it from him at an early age.

5. Is he / she one of your favourite dogs of all time?

Serious will always be one of my favourite dogs of all time. He is the dog who has made me the trainer I am today. He holds a very special place in my heart.

6. What is his / her favourite activity?

Serious' favourite activity was playing ball and going for a swim often.

7. What is his / her biggest achievements?

This is a hard question for me to answer as Serious' biggest achievement personally for me would be every single trial that he has participated in. This dog was heavily tested from the age of 6 months. He beat and also ran alongside seasoned dogs his whole puppyhood. This is not something I'm proud of and/or want to gloat about, mainly the reason for this was me being an inexperienced handler with such a good puppy however you live and you learn and we sure did.

He was the youngest dog to ever win a Level 3 Trial in the UK and still holds the record until this day (aged 16 months). He had a number of achievements which included;
- NASDU Level 2
- NIPDT
- Lorockmor Level 3 Winner
- Lorockmor Long Send Winner
- AVD Silver Class Winner (X2)
- AVD Bronze Class Winner
- APPDA Entry Level
- Fright Trials Sleeve Winner

- HK9 Street Readiness Pass

8. Was he / she difficult to train?

Serious wasn't really difficult to train in the early years however as he became more mature and testosterone kicked in, he became a bit of a knucklehead.

9. What's your favourite offspring of his / her?

My favourite offspring of Serious' would be Diva. Reason being is the fact that she is a lot like him in many ways, more so out of drive, dominant characteristics and willing to do anything.

10. How heavy was or is he / she?

He is currently 80lbs.

11. Where is your training club and decoys who helped him / her?

Our training club is in Essex, UK - Britannia K9 Training Academy. The decoys who helped with the development of Serious would be Danny Lines & Scott Bullvision.

12. If you have the same dog again, what will you so different?

If I had another Serious, I would take things a lot slower and would have taken him the sport route instead ie KNPV system which we did dibble and dabble in as he knew some of the routines.

13. Is he / she social with people?

Serious is socially acceptant. He can be in social situations i.e. large crowds as he was a demonstration dog for Britannia on many occasions and also a security dog on the streets of London. Oh, and enjoyed walks in the park feeding the ducks with the kids.

15. If you can change 1 thing about the dog, what would it be?

One thing I would change about Serious would be his spinning. Sometimes watching him would make me feel dizzy.

16. How was the dog like when he/ she as a puppy?

Serious was 100% the best puppy I've ever owned. He was clean from day one with no accidents even when he had a bad belly. He was very forward and always acted more mature than what he actually was.

17. How was he / she like as he / she matured?

When Serious matured he was a very easy dog to have, sometimes you would forget that he was even there partly the reason why I sold him to America. As when you train a lot of dogs, you tend to forget the quiet easy going dogs that can do anything that's asked of them and focus more on the disobedient ones.

18. How are the dog's litter mates?

Serious is out of a litter of 14. However we only really stayed in contact with 2 other owners. From what we saw, they were very much consistent like him.

19. Is he / she social with other dogs?

Serious is social with other dogs as long as they never show dominance over him. He did have a lot more tolerance towards puppies.

20. Does the dog live in a house or a kennel?

Serious has lived in both outdoors and indoors.

Dog 93 – Judo (AKC DN40285104)

Owner: Joseph Cinnante

1. How is he / she at home, out of work?

Judo is the ideal dog when he's not working. He's completely fine with just laying around, relaxing with our kids. He's also the best travel partner I've ever had. I can leave him in hotel rooms or foreign households alone all day and he never causes a problem.

2. Describe his or her character with 5 words..

He's extremely socially and environmentally sound.

3. What is his / her best quality?

In my opinion Judo's best quality is his intensity. He puts everything into his work, often sacrificing his own safety. Whether it be jumping or in protection work, every time you pull the trigger and 'send him' there is the potential for an extremely explosive event.

4. What is his / her least desirable attribute?

Part of what makes Judo such a spectacular animal is also potentially part of his downfall. Along with the speed and power he brings, his lack of self preservation has taken its toll on his body. As a result, we've had to retire him from competition at the young age of 5 year old.

5. Is he / she one of your favourite dogs of all time?

He is absolutely one of my favorite dogs and without a doubt my most appreciated teacher ever.

6. What is his / her favourite activity?

His favorite activities are eating food, biting and really anything that involves intent physicality. He's a complete bull.

7. What is his / her biggest achievements?

Judo's biggest achievement in my opinion was bouncing back from a significant injury, and after over a year off competing for a season in France. He won a Regional Championship there and put up some very impressive scores against very experienced Finalist dogs and French Champions.

8. Was he / she difficult to train?

I don't think he was difficult to train, but as he matured he became more challenging to control. He taught me more than I can express when it comes to trial preparation.

9. What's your favourite offspring of his / her?

We never bred Judo. He has some health issues that I didn't want to risk passing down through his offspring.

10. How heavy was or is he / she?

Judo's competition weight was a lean 70lbs. He could easily walk around at 75lbs and look fit as well.

11. Where is your training club and decoys who helped him / her?

We didn't belong to a training club. A lot of Judo' foundation was laid with my friend Oscar Mora. And we worked alone a lot so we were forced to improvise. As far as his return after the hiatus due to his injury, it was my friend Fabrice Pouzens who helped me prepare him for competition in France.

12. If you have the same dog again, what will you so different?

I would be much more careful with his body as I was developing him. I can't help but think that I contributed to his body breaking down early by not being as careful as I should have been.

13. Is he / she social with people?

He is very social. But is also very capable and equipped to destroy a person if needed.

14. Any funny stories you want to share?

When he was under a year old and I hadn't acclimated him fully to in-home living yet, he spent a lot of down time in his crate. One night around the Christmas holidays I went to a neighbor's house for drinks. I was sure I put him in his crate, but I'm not sure I ever actually secured the door. When I returned home, I saw Judo standing at the door, breathing extremely heavily on the glass and wagging his tail excitedly. I was struck immediately both with confusion and concern. When I opened the door I saw that Judo had torn up every single gift that was under the tree. You couldn't even see the floor because it was covered in wrapping paper and shredded gifts. Needless to say, that may have been one of the best days of Judo's life.

15. If you can change 1 thing about the dog, what would it be?

His physical health. If I had a time machine I would go back and take much better care of him in hopes of achieving a longer career for him.

16. How was the dog like when he/ she as a puppy?

He was a stunning looking pup. Big boned and strong. In the work he was always fast, but not over the top impressive in any area. In fact I almost sold him before he was a year old. My friend Tony Moucheghian came to California from France to do a seminar, and after working Judo for a week convinced me to not sell him. I can't thank him enough for that.

17. How was he / she like as he / she matured?

Judo matured beautifully. Between 1 & 2 years old he made a lot of changes. He grew a ton physically and mentally. But between 2 & 3 years old he changed even more. I often say that in that year he became a little lion.

18. How are the dog's litter mates?

A number of the males in the litter turned out really strong. Most of them were a bit angrier and less social than Judo. One of his sisters achieved her French Ring 3 title, and one of his brothers is currently competing in French Ring at Level 3.

19. Is he / she social with other dogs?

He is very social with and tolerant of most dogs. Judo helps us work with a lot of reactive and aggressive dogs in order to help them with their social issues.

20. Does the dog live in a house or a kennel?

Judo has always lived in the houser with us. Once he was fully acclimated to in-home living there was no longer any need for a crate. We also have outdoor enclosures that we use for all of our dogs so that they can get some sun, fresh air and relax outside safely.

Dog 94 – Jochie (BRN15819)

Owner: Chris Race

Recount: Johnny Ulrich
Translated by Marcel Aalders and Emily Houk

Jochie was bred by Bert Hendrix and was born September 20, 2008. He is out of the combination, Tessa Hendrix x Rico Hendrix. This combination brought many prolific dogs. Some notable siblings of Jochie from this combination are: Rico Vergossen, Rico te Lindert, Kwinto Sommers, and Noa te Lindert.

Jochie was purchased as a puppy by Johnny Ulrich. Johnny trained Jochie within the KNPV program with the help of Peter Sommers and Thijs Heinhuis. Johnny says without the help of these two men, certifying Jochie never would've been possible.

Jochie was a very stubborn, and very very hard dog. Marcel notes, he's one of the hardest dogs he's ever seen. He also had a ton of drive, and absolutely no self-preservation. All these things combined made it difficult to get the dog certified. As Johnny says, Jochie was a beast on the field and he spent numerous nights awake because of Jochie; trying to figure out ways to teach him the exercises. They trained 3-4 times per week with Jochie, and in the end he managed to get his PH1 certification with a score of 424 CL.

As difficult a dog as he was during training, he was completely different outside of work. Johnny says, this is one of the things that made him so special. At home, he was the sweetest dog in the world, especially with Johnny's children. He was social, affectionate, just an all-around nice house dog.

Chris Race and Marcel Aalders purchased Jochie before certification but made arrangements for him to not be shipped until after certification. After certification, Jochie flew to Chris Race in Florida. This is where Jochie stayed for the rest of his life. Jochie meant more to Chris than words can describe.

Dog 95 - Charlie van der Doelen (BRN8764)

Owner: Tini van der Doelen

Translated by Marcel Aalders and Emily Houk

Charlie was bred by John Willems (born January 19th, 2004). He came from a litter of six males and three females. Of the 9 puppies, seven certified with a PH1. Charlie was purchased as a puppy by Sjaak Verhaaren. Sjaak raised and trained Charlie to achieve around 12 certificates/titles in total. This of course also includes up to his IPO3 as well as numerous tracking/searching certificates in IPO and KNPV. Charlie was also fully trained and prepared for his PH1 certificate. Unfortunately, Charlie's handler passed away before going for his PH1. After Sjaaks passing, Charlie was purchased by Tini van der Doelen. Charlie stayed here with Tini until he died.

Charlie was a typical one man's dog. He was in a way, loyal to a fault to his handler. He was social to where strangers could be around with Tini present and he wouldn't just bite someone. But he would follow Tini everywhere and stay by him. Charlie was the type of dog who was always prepared to protect, but wouldn't do it without a legitimate reason. Charlie's son, Max Doelen, shares these characteristics in the same manner.

Charlie was also an extremely good searcher. The type of dog who searches for the search, not what is at the end or for the reward. The search itself was the reward for Charlie. He also produces this in a dominant way.

Charlie was also a great producer across the board and notoriously makes a good combination with the Duco lines. This combination typically brings out the good of both sides, without taking anything away. Some notable offspring of Charlie include, Celiks Home Bono (BRN 19028), Blaze (BRN 25658), Max (BRN 33786), Condor (BRN 25706), Ammie (BRN 22384), Celiks Home Kaat (BRN 30361), and Freddy (BRN 19674).

Charlie serving pica.

Dog 96 – Akuma

Owner: Jared Wolf

1. How is he / she at home, out of work?

Akuma lives the working dog and pet lifestyle so he's out of his kennel hanging out when I'm at home with him and he is very well behaved.

2. Describe his or her character with 5 words..

Powerful, playful, intelligent, affectionate and clever.

3. What is his / her best quality?

I'd say the fact that he's such a balanced dog. He has two very different sides to him.

4. What is his / her least desirable attribute?

I don't have anything negative to say about him.

5. Is he / she one of your favourite dogs of all time?

Definitely!

6. What is his / her favourite activity?

Bitework !

7. What are his / her biggest achievements?

PSA1 1 leg so far we are trialing in a few weeks for our second leg then getting ready for nationals.

8. Was he / she difficult to train?

There's always going to be obstacles but he's been a lot of fun.

9. What's your favourite offspring of his / her?

He hasn't been bred yet.

10. How heavy was or is he / she?

2 years old.

11. Where is your training club and decoys who helped him / her?

Nomad working dogs. Decoys Josh Knowlton, Stefan herceg, jacob Walthall and Steve Roberts.

12. If you have the same dog again, what will you do differently?

I wouldn't change anything about our training. We are on the right track right now !

13. Is he / she social with people?

He's a very social dog !

14. Any funny stories you want to share?

N/A.

15. If you can change 1 thing about the dog, what would it be?

Nothing!

16. How was the dog like when he/ she was a puppy?

Very confident and pretty high energy. He's definitely calmed down around the time he turned 2.

17. How was he / she like as he / she matured?

He's still pretty young but he's just getting more serious about his work.

18. How are the dog's litter mates?

His litter mates are all very nice dogs that also compete in the sport of PSA.

19. Is he / she social with other dogs?

He's a social dog but if another male challenges he doesn't take kindly to that.

20. Does the dog live in a house or a kennel?

He lives with me at my loft.

Dog 97 – Finn (BRN29507)

Owner: Leos Drbohlav

1. How is he / she at home, out of work?

At the house he is very chill and relaxed, however when he steps outside the house whether it is just to potty or even going in a car, he is 100% alert and ready. On longer rides he goes back to relax mode.

2. Describe his or her character with 5 words..

Intense, fast, no quitter, strong and warrior.

3. What is his / her best quality?

Has plenty of natural aggression. Loves to fight anyone anytime anywhere. His searching ability is off the charts as well. Extremely good nose. His adaptability is second to none as well. Whether it is flying a helicopter or water or repelling he adapts to anything really fast.

4. What is his / her least desirable attribute?

Always going 1000 miles per min!

5. Is he / she one of your favourite dogs of all time?

I have trained or worked with well over 1000 dogs and worked in field and owned 7 LE/Mil dogs in my life. Finn is definitely the most favorite dog ever gone through my hands.

6. What is his / her favourite activity?

Trying to kill something at all times. Whether it is a branch, a log or a bottle or something. He is always pissed at something and killing it till it is taken apart. Then he finds something else to be pissed at.

7. What are his / her biggest achievements?

Finn is a law enforcement certified K9 for Narcotics and Apprehension but also SWAT/Special Warfare Tactics K9.

8. Was he / she difficult to train?

When I got Finn he was just a nerve ball. I had to rebuild his entire perception of the world but then he became a very fast learner.

9. What's your favourite offspring of his / her?

Finn x Atlanta van Quest (phenomenal dogs in every way with lots of natural aggression. Old school type of dogs).

10. How heavy is he / she?

65 pounds.

11. Where is your training club and decoys who helped him / her?

Don't have any.

12. If you have the same dog again, what will you do differently?

Nothing, he is absolutely perfect!

13. Is he / she social with people?

He doesn't care for people. If people try to pet him he just runs around like they don't exist. He doesn't really care for anyone touching him but me.

14. Any funny stories you want to share?

One day he got lost in a building and couldn't find his way to me so he jumped off from the second floor to get to me. I rushed him to emergency and when we got there he first pissed on the flower bed in front of the building and then he started to sniff the whole clinic for narcotics and I couldn't stop him from doing that. (He was absolutely fine, not a single damage on his body).

15. If you can change 1 thing about the dog, what would it be?

Nothing.

16. What was the dog like when he/ she as a puppy?

I got him when he was 7 months old. By then he went through 3 different owners. He was a special case.

17. How was he / she like as he / she matured?

Same nut case as young except stronger and trained so he can be in a civilized world now.

18. How are the dog's litter mates?

I only knew of one brother and he was put down for being aggressive to people.

19. Is he / she social with other dogs?

Yes he doesn't care about any animals in general.

20. Does the dog live in a house or a kennel?

Lives outside but comes to the house often.

Dog 98 – Hanzo (BRN29418)

Owner: Andrea S Taher

1. How is he / she at home, out of work?

Hanzo is chilled in the kennel but alert at all times, he guards his kennel well and will bark if he hears someone on the driveway. The moment he's out the kennel he is bouncing around and ready to work.

2. Describe his or her character with 5 words..

Intense, dominant, pushy, stubborn and self assured.

3. What is his / her best quality?

His explosiveness in his work, often people assume he's really calm and controlled then he will explode in drive, make mistakes or redirects. He's gotten a lot better with age (now 5) with clarity in the work.

He is well tested in his ability to take mental and physical pressure from handler / second handler. When I say he is handler hard, I dont judge it when a dog is being corrected while high in drive. At this age he is still being corrected for things such as refusing to out the ball and he still makes the same mistakes occasionally. He can also take decoy pressure throughout the years in different stages of the various work I've put him through especially in the early days puppy till 2.5 years old. He was tested thoroughly in all sorts of new scenarios that I never trained for.

His courage or stubbornness. In the KNPV program, he knows the routine and what is expected of him and knows full well he will get corrected if he makes these mistakes. However it's almost as if he's willing to take the punishment to get what he wants.

Hanzo's dumbness can be a blessing and a curse. Often he is very impulsive and will do things before even thinking, always diving head first.

A lot of people only see him on the field but those that know him out of work see how he's like. Although he is neutral, he has an edge, always alert and walks with a sense of self assertiveness. He will not hesitate to grow and let you know he's not pleased.

Our club have nicknamed him the hammer because although he's not a large dog, he often takes decoys down even in Holland! Saying that I do worry he will injure him badly, he's had a few sprains throughout training.

4. What is his / her least desirable attribute?

Could be genetics or due to my lack of knowledge on developing grips but I've always been honest to anyone who's asked. It's his grips and bite mechanics. It is the only thing that's lacking in him.

5. Is he / she one of your favourite dogs of all time?

We have quite a few dogs and they all have things I like and dislike. Hanzo will definitely be difficult to replace and I hope his son Chief will surpass his dad in every way.

6. What is his / her favourite activity?

Long hikes in the countryside or holiday, ball fetch and training.

7. What is his / her biggest achievements?

His biggest achievement is yet to come which is his PH1. Due to corona it's delayed us almost 2 years. Over the years he's achieved APPDA entry level, night trial long send sleeve first place, coming top 10 in many trials and being worked by decoys all over the country and from USA.

He was tested from day one and proved to be able to handle both handler pressure abs decoy pressure. It was a difficult transition from the crazy bitework to KNPV and the first 18 months was super tough on him but he took it and thrived as he always does!

8. Was he / she difficult to train?

I would say so, he needed an experienced handler for sure. Without the help of other trainers I wouldn't be able to get to where we are now!

His high drive allows him to learn things easily however his stubbornness and hard headedness as well as redirection issues made it very difficult at the start. Now he still makes rookie mistakes because he couldn't help himself and often training is like a rollercoaster. Really tests my patience as a handler for sure. He is very intense in his work and often goes from super calm to explosive of fury within the split of a second and sometimes that aggression clouds his clarity and our Dutch mentors called it his red zone.

9. What's your favourite offspring of his / her?

He only had 2 litters. First litter, the pups are 12 months old and I keep track of them, one is doing IPG and the other as a PPD. He's thrown his phenotype but bigger and also his balanced nature, high energy, hardness, pushiness in them.

Second litter is proving to be really promising. We have Chief, other one Blitz in UK doing KNPV and the other 2 in USA planning to do PSA. Chief so far is highly driven, high energy, solid nerve, pushy, can take handler pressure and flammable as well as showing his stubbornness like his dad. The other pups are all high energy, high drive and solid nerves.

Both litters have Hanzo's looks and he definitely threw size (all pups are giants), his hardness, recovery and character.

10. How heavy was or is he / she?

He ranges between 33kg to 36kg.

11. Where is your training club and decoys who helped him / her?

So many to name.. but currently it's PHV Herten in Holland and our club PHV Lorockmor. Some of the top trainers and decoys in Holland such as Erwin Coolen, Jack Delissen, Andy Boyen and Danny Giessen. In UK, Ian Morgan, Sam Frost, Laurie Stanley and Asa Wright.

In the past, Scott Bullvision trained him in the early days as well as Brittania K9.

12. If you have the same dog again, what will you do differently?

Although I don't regret I've tested him extensively from such a young age, I would definitely work in his grips and bite mechanics first.

13. Is he / she social with people?

He is neutral to people but if over aroused, he will growl and will bite if anyone tries to do things to him.

14. Any funny stories you want to share?

He is a pain in the butt at the vets even muzzled. He had to get a minor surgery and I've told the vets we will restrain at the car park to be sedated first. The vet said no they'll be ok, as I mentioned before he often gives a false sense of security. The vets and Hanzo trotted into the vets office then we proceeded to drive 2 hours to go training.

When we arrived to training I got a phone call from the vets to say he is trying to kill them even with a muzzle and having 3 staff members try to pin him down. They then left him in the kennel and gave him some food!! I was like "told you so". So we had to go back the next day while me and Muz handled him, he did try his luck but we won the battle.

Another story is similar but with semen collection. He went crazy in a muzzle while being collected so both me and Muz had to have a conversation prior. Needless to say he had an angry wank and low volume of sperm that day!

15. If you can change 1 thing about the dog, what would it be?

Previously mentioned, his grips and bite mechanics.

16. How was the dog like when he/ she as a puppy?

I had him at 16 weeks. He came from rural farmlands to busy London City. Nothing phased him, he was very independent and cool as a cucumber, not an affectionate puppy. I had to work hard on engagement.

17. How was he / she like as he / she matured?

As Hanzo matured, his aggression issues like kennel guarding, redirecting and pushiness also came. It was round about 10/11 months old. I worked him heavy in obedience and control. He thrives on conflict of any sort be it with handler, decoy or other dogs.

18. How are the dog's litter mates?

One brother is in the Dutch Air Force, the other one was doing KNPV until he bit the handler badly and was sold to USA, now he is a PD.

19. Is he / she social with other dogs?

He is neutral and often works around dogs with 0 reactivity, however he does not tolerate any adult dog coming up to him. Female or male doesn't matter, if they come up to his face, without warning he will go for them. It's happened a few times.

During mating, he has to be muzzled. Even when the female showed submission he was very aggressive.

But with puppies he is fantastic! I trust him the most when it comes to puppies and young dogs (younger than 9 months old). He lets them rag his neck or tail and pretty much ignores them.

20. Does the dog live in a house or a kennel?

Only in a kennel with no bedding but a thick horse mat. He destroys everything otherwise.

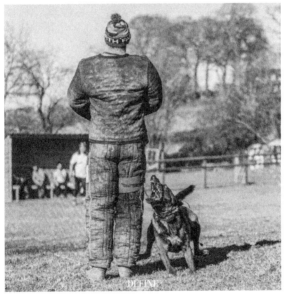

Dog 99 – Demon (BRN29508)

Owner: Mus Taher

Demon was an accidental purchase! Bred by Hein Van Gaalen who also bred Hanzo, our trip out to Holland was to pick up Hanzo, who Andrea had planned to buy and work with. As we were leaving the kennels Danny Lines and Hein came out with 2 pups and all I could hear and see was a commotion from 5 meters away Demon and his litter brother were fighting and in separating them one had latched on to Hein's jumper the other Danny's leg! When put into the crate, he was screaming and biting at the kennel bars to come out. I fell in love instantly.

When we arrived in London we tested him inside Danny's garden shed with disco lights on a rag. He grabbed onto it with little to no movement and wouldn't let go. Being lifted in the air, slapped side to side and screamed at. This little black pup was possessed! Demon, who was supposed to be Danny's pup, became my pup right there and then!

As Demon hit 8 weeks old he showed signs of defensive aggression towards people wanting to run up to them and bite them. It was almost impossible to socialise him as a pup as his initial reaction was to bite. People would run away and as a result would reward his bad behaviour inadvertently. This was something I had never experienced before with a young pup.

He was very self assured in all environments and is one of his most incredible traits. His nerve is rock solid. But people are not his friends. He wanted to start trouble, always looking for who he could bite. By 3 months old he had bitten the cleaner in my office, a woman on the street, chased some kids in a park and bit a few of my work colleagues. He was truly out of control and only a few weeks old.

My mistakes compounded with him as instead of stopping bite work I carried on and my inexperience ment I didn't correct the trainers who worked him in defence quite often. As a result he was unbearable and as he approached teething he could not be taken out around strangers. The final nail in the coffin was when we were in a busy crowd of people and he triggered into drive to bite everyone in the way with nowhere for me to go but onto incoming busy traffic.

Something had to change. We then decided to start to heavily correct him which we wanted to avoid with such a young pup. Almost every encounter with someone new meant he would be corrected heavily as soon as he showed signs of aggression. We stopped all defensive work and stopped all work that would get him into a heightened state of arousal. The corrections meant he learned to avoid the people rather than to engage them to avoid the corrections, even though this is not what most people in security would want, for me it was perfect. I preferred him to avoid than to engage which would surely lead to a costly lawsuit or worse the destruction of the dog once older.

By 1 Demon had structure and had learned to be a more tolerant dog of people. His bitework was scripted and he knew when it's ok to bite (when the harness is on) and when it's not acceptable to be aggressive and bite (pinch collar, flat or grot). As the months went on he showed incredible resilience to his early poor foundations and continues to thrive.

He is a very environmentally strong dog. My early recollection of him going through firework stations and smoke stations that seasoned adults didn't want to do always resides with me. I have to date never seen Demon wary of a new environment.

He is an extremely athletic dog with incredible grace, speed and stride. His bite is hard and full and possessive. He always impresses in all new stations and bites. Jumping through obstacles, never slowing down or hesitating and flying into the unknown or launching into targets, Demon loves to bite.

He has an incredibly strong nose and hunt drive. Methodical, calm and very driven to use his nose. Over the years he has become an accidental celebrity and my "stunt dog" for crazy action shots and building the following of MuzMuzTV and MuzMuzMutz. He has become one of the most recognisable dogs from videos I've shared of him working. He truly is an impressive dog to watch in action.

Demon is one of the most loyal dogs to his pack. I will always be grateful to own such a difficult dog as Demon was in his early days as he made me a much better handler, trainer and dog man.

Demon has not been bred yet as we have to make sure a female can balance that sharpness out. Demon weighs around 34KG lean. He loves to swim and dock dive but nothing compares to bitework when it comes to his favourite activity!

If I can do it all again with Demon I would but knowing what I know now he would be a different dog and I would have enforced a harder set of structures much earlier into him. I would own him again in a heartbeat. Walking alone in the dark, Demon will give you that sense of security naturally. Chest out, alert and ready for anything that comes his way. He is very easy to get into drive for work and I regard him as very very high drive for bitework. High food & ball drive with an equally high defence and prey drive.

As I spent so long working on making him suitable for my life, I ignored making him suitable for sports and trials. In reality I have held the dog back in fear of regressing him back to an unbearable unbalanced out of control dog on a day to day basis like he was when a young dog. This is my biggest regret and I wish I had spent more time earlier setting better foundations and rules.

His biggest achievement is founding MuzMuzTV! Without Demon I wouldnt have thought to reach out to more trainers and learn from them, or to see how others work their dogs, or to be interested in bloodlines and the different subtle balances in what makes working dogs. Without Demon, and the challenges he posed while training him as a young pup, MuzMuzTV would never have been formed. MuzMuzTV was alwasy a way for us to reach more people and connect with them and Demon was incremental in the reason for that.

A natural personal protection dog first with the stardust on his feet to warrant his celebrity!

Dog 100 - Ra's Al Ghul (BRN37998 / LOSH1282017)

Owner: Mus Taher

At the time of writing Ra's Al Ghul is 2.5 years old in training for KNPV Ph1. Ra's is one of the most extreme driven dogs I have seen and is extremely possessive in whatever he has in his mouth. Be it small articles, copper pipe, ball or bite. On the other side of the coin he is one of the most chilled, unreactive and stable dogs I know. He is able to relax or go on walks without reacting to animals, dogs or people. He is confident in whatever new environment I take him to and is a very very easy dog to live with.

To best describe his character I will share a few experiences I have had with him that will hopefully demonstrate the kind of dog he is.

First Water Experience!

Ra's was maybe 4 months old, we had just collected him from Belgium and we went to meet our Dutch mentors in Holland at a local fast water flowing canal to practice the water exercises with Hanzo for PH1 training. I decided to take Ra's out the van as a puppy to meet everyone after the work was finished at the banks of the river. He met everyone with his customary wagging tail and proceeded to run head first into the fast flowing canal where water was flowing through guards effectively creating a waterfall effect. In my head panic set in. I was sure he would either get swept away, get injured if he hit the railings or have such a bad experience that he would never want to swim again. He somehow managed to swim to the bank of the canal and we fished him out after close to a minute of him swimming around in circles. After coming out he shook the water off and ran round doing a zoomie and the crazy Asshat dived head first back into the canal!! I knew then he was a little special pup!

First time Holding keys!

Ra's hadn't seen the keys until he reached around 1 or so years old. We simply never thought of training it. So one evening we held a bunch of keys (no winding up), had him in a sit and threw the keys 3 meters ahead of him and asked him to bring them back. He grabbed the keys, ran back at super speed and just clamped through the keys into his tongue, calm and not chomping all the while bleeding into the keys as they dug into his cheeks and tongue and not letting go. He clamped so hard on them he ripped into his own tongue. We have ever since had problems with him clean outing on the keys and has been one of the hardest exercises to train him on. His possession is so high it gets hard for him to calmly release the keys which regularly results in aggression directed towards the handler or the object. Too much of something is not always a good thing!

The 45 minute bite!

Ra's is an extremely impressive animal on the bite. He has amazing stamina to just bite. No agitation or stimulation is needed for him. He doesn't care about decoy feedback. He just wants to carry on biting even when the decoy is stationary and still or passive. We tested this with my close friend Scott Bullvision. Ra's was on the bicep bite for a good 45 minutes with no change in his mechanics or positioning. The only reason we took him off in the end was Scott had enough! I think he could have stayed there the whole day! He was exhausted but just stayed full mouthed, countering and possessing the bite.

First ever bite with us!

Before Ra's we had gone through 10 other pups that didn't work out. We were quite disheartened and as such when we picked him up at 4 months from Belgium we didn't have much expectations. Infact on the first night we had him we arrived in Holland and asked one of our mentors to "test" if he's any good. We trained Hanzo first until around 10 pm and left the young pup Ra's back tied alone in the dark on the other field until we finished. Our mentor went into the cabin, took a sleeve, a large canister & a KNPV stick. It was quite dark and our mentor walked up to the dog with almost no stim, no prey movements and no soft breaking in. He screamed at Ra's as he got to about 1 meter away, hit the KNPV stick on either side of him and smashed the canister on the ground in front of him. Ra's almost instinctively hit the end of the chain screaming back in an almost primitive scream, I was just an observer now. He bit the sleeve, grabbed it full mouth and was silent on the bite. My mentor asked me to choke him off after 30 seconds. As he hit the ground he screamed at the end of the line for the bite to come back as the trainer walked away and said put the dog back in the car. When I went into the cabin I asked him what he thought. He said a handful of words: "He's a Good Dog Muz"! I knew he was special there and then!

In total Ra's is an extremely highly driven Malinois with exceptional energy levels and a possessive nature. His possession does however, sometimes make him lose clarity and has a tendency to redirect at the handler. In his first 2 years of training he had many "come to Jesus" moments with me and I've always admired his ability to dust himself off and carry on wanting to work like nothing happened. For me that's one of his most impressive traits.

He is my dream dog. Totally calm and relaxed and reliable out of work. He is not reactive or aggressive to people or dogs or animals but at the drop of a hat he is able to go super saiyan level drive and intensity. It is very rare to find an animal that can be both.

As a puppy he was perfect. I couldn't hope for a better pup. Everything he was introduced to he did. At 4 months we did 2 or 3 sleeve bites on his biceps and then he was on a full suit on multiple decoys. He has bitten some of the biggest name decoys in Europe and all have had good feedback on what they thought of him.

He is not a suspicious dog and if I can change anything about him I would wish he was a little bigger. He weighs 28/29KG and keeps lean and as a result no matter how fast he comes into the bite he rarely takes the decoys down! Another 5 KG and he would be a nightmare for helpers at full speed.

Ra's has only had 2 sons when bred to Lorocmor Viper. Flash and Pyro. At the time of writing they are both very nice young 11 week old pups. Full of drive, energy and desire to bite and work. He will be bred to select females in the future and we are quite confident he will throw drive and high energy levels when mated.

Ra's lives in a giant air crate in a kennel. His litter brothers and sisters are all working and some are due to be titled soon. If I owned the dog again the only thing I would change is preserve him from injury as he has suffered a few over the past year which although have not been catastrophic have ment long periods out of action in recovery and that has slowed our progress for PH1.

I would own Ra's over and again for the rest of my life. He's my best friend and makes me proud every time I have worked him. Difficult dog to work because of his extreme drive, possession and tendency to redirect, but I wouldn't change anything about him!